SHARK
MAN

Theo Ferreira

SUNBIRD
PUBLISHERS

First published 2007

2 4 6 8 1 0 9 7 5 3 1

Sunbird Publishers (Pty) Ltd
PO Box 6836, Roggebaai 8012
Cape Town, South Africa

www.sunbirdpublishers.co.za

Registration number: 4850177827

Publisher: Natanya Mulholland
Editor: Willem Steenkamp
Proofreader: Sean Fraser
Production Manager: Andrew de Kock

Reproduction by Resolution Colour (Pty) Ltd, Cape Town
Printed and bound by Paarl Print

10 digit ISBN: 1-919938-64-8
13 digit ISBN: 978-1-919938-64-6

DEDICATION

I dedicate the true story of my lifelong roller-coaster ride with the great white shark to the most reliable, supportive, loyal and brave-hearted person ever to touch my life: my beautiful, loving, gentle wife and allround best friend, Norma, who rode along with me almost from the beginning, only to pass away before I could complete this account.

NOTE OF THANKS

Although I am the author of this book, I am by no means the sole contributor. Many others played an integral role in my long, frequently difficult and often dangerous involvement with great white sharks, which supplied the experiences and knowledge that gave rise to what I have written here.

To mention each one would be a formidable task, and I would run the risk of leaving some out. So I shall give thanks by name in some cases and in general to all the rest.

My particular thanks for their unwavering commitment go to the people closest to the sharp end: my son Craig, who was initiated into the world of the great white shark at the tender age of 13, and my daughters Tracy and Cherie, and also to all the assistants and volunteers who helped to make the White Shark Research Project (of which more later) work over the recent and more distant past.

Our involvement with great white sharks has taken us all over the world, to dive shows, universities, expos and dive clubs, where we have presented lectures on our experiences and the knowledge we have gained. Thanks to all of the people involved – and of course my wife Norma, who played a full role in these activities – I have an opportunity to lead you into the wondrous and amazing world of the great white shark.

CONTENTS

PREFACE

The vast plains of Africa are rightly famous for the Big Five that still roam them in spite of the depredations of poachers: the regal lion, the elusive leopard, the earth-shaking elephant, the hair-trigger-tempered buffalo and the unstoppable rhino. Awesome in appearance and ferocity when aroused, they have inspired an immense treasure-trove of fact, myth and legend in the minds of humans who heed the call of the wild and see them in their natural state.

But the most fearsome of all the animals of Africa does not dwell on land. It lives in the depths off its coast and it is called *Carcharodon carcharias* – or, as we intruders into its dim blue jungle usually call it, the 'great white shark', or just 'white shark'.

The white shark holds the copyright on human fear because all the odds are on its side. Man is a land animal, like the Big Five, and when he tangles with them he can employ all his natural strength and cunning in the milieu in which he is the most familiar. But in the white shark's world he is an intruder, feebly equipped to fight for his life, never mind to win, and so all the odds are against him.

Carcharodon carcharias is nature's most formidable and efficient predator, a finely tuned precision-killing machine. Your evolutionist will explain the perfection of the white shark in straightforward Darwinian terms, but some people who know it as well as I do find it hard to attribute such perfection in every detail and ability to mere chance. Even a die-hard cynic might find himself conceding that a creature as perfect as this must have had a supreme designer and creator.

That is a large statement to make in this disbelieving world, but let me share with you the amazing adventure that I have been privileged to experience – and tell you the story that has not yet ended, even if the main character is no longer myself but the next generation.

It is not my intention to interpret how the white shark thinks and why it behaves the way it does. Instead I will share with you what I have experienced and observed over the years, and let you decide for yourself whether or not I am overstating the case.

INTRODUCTION

I am no bunny-hugging conservationist who feels diminished when he accidentally steps on an insect. I became an admirer of great white sharks the hard way: for years I was an inveterate and very successful hunter of great whites. Then I turned full circle and became their protector.

I don't regret that first phase, because I know now that it was part of a long educational process that turned me into a more complete and informed individual. I feel very privileged to have been afforded the opportunity to learn from and interact with these complex and mighty creatures on their terms. It has made me realise that these apex predators form a vital link in our ecosystem and that they should be recognised as an asset to life on earth, rather than as an enemy of humankind.

This doesn't mean that I have gone starry-eyed, however. I love sharks and I love being out on the ocean with them, but I am not going to tell you that they are cute. 'Cute' is not a word that you use in the same breath as 'shark'. The big predators among the species – the white, the tiger, the Zambezi and several others – are very dangerous indeed.

But there is no malice to them, and it serves no purpose to demonise them. Sharks are not evil, any more than an earthquake is evil; if they were, we would be in serious trouble. In point of fact, they are neutral, simply an elemental force of nature.

Films like *Jaws* to the contrary, they are not man-eaters by preference or possessed by thoughts of revenge. They are, rather, very complex animals with an important ecological role, and when one of them attacks a human being it is no more than a case of someone being in the wrong place at the wrong time.

This is the anatomy of a typical shark attack:

The female shark cruises slowly along at a depth of about seven metres, her smooth white belly almost brushing the bottom, stirring up little tornadoes of fine silt as her great tail sweeps from side to side. She is gigantic, five metres long and weighing almost 1 360 kilos, and as she glides silently over the white sand and tufts of sea-grass the lesser ocean animals of her domain swim panic-stricken for cover. But they are in no danger: she is after greater game than small fish and other marine creatures.

As the water becomes shallower she changes her course, so that she is cruising parallel to the shore with its rumbling surf, some 200 metres away. The terrain has changed along with the direction, and she is forced to angle her body towards the surface to avoid the reef and pinnacles of rock now obstructing her path. She levels out at about a metre from the surface, which is calm except for a low swell gently running towards the beach.

This part of the ocean is familiar to her. She often patrols these shores in search of the skates and rays congregating to breed here during the summer months. But the rays are late this year, and she has not caught one since the day before. So now she is sneaking up on one of the seal colonies she knows.

The shark reaches a bay, and changes course once more to follow the contours of the coastline. She knows that usually the rays are to be found here, scavenging in the shallows close to the shore, so she turns towards the beach. Little outcrops of rock pass under her belly as she follows the gentle shelving of the seabed towards the beach, now not more than about 150 metres away. But it is a bad year, and there are no rays to be found.

She has just levelled off, parallel to the shore, when the line of minute sensors and pores in her hide prickles as it detects the pressure-signals sent by a rhythmic thumping near the surface, a mere 100 metres away. The shark immediately slows even more, till she hangs almost motionless in the water while her senses collect more information about the source of the disturbance.

The thumping suddenly stops; but her interest has been aroused by now, and she angles towards the area in the hope of picking it up again. She has only covered about 30 metres when the thumping resumes; her highly developed pressure sensory system allows her to pinpoint the precise location and approximate size of the animal that is emitting the signals.

She has encountered these signals before, so they are not completely alien to her. But till now she has never investigated them, because her instinct for survival has prompted her to avoid the unknown, and they have always come from the surf, where she does not like to go.

But she is very hungry, so hungry that her immediate need overcomes her built-in caution and drives her to explore the possibility that the alien signals might emanate from something worth eating.

Carefully, she closes in. The author of the disturbance is only metres behind the surf-zone, and when a large wave breaks, the rhythmic signals momentarily disappear. The shark keeps moving despite her instinctive fear of shallow water, because her built-in computer tells her that if the prey moves into the surf itself, it will be very difficult to locate and dangerous to pursue, and her ever more urgent hunger will not let her turn back now.

When she is barely 15 metres away the prey falls silent again, and the shark changes tactics, veering away from her direct course and swimming with her belly almost touching the bottom to avoid detection in the shallows. But the moment for caution is almost over: soon it will be time to attack. She is so close now that she can see the prey silhouetted on the surface of the water. Adrenaline starts pumping through her veins as she prepares herself for the final attack.

The great shark flicks her tail a few times to gain some speed and glides past the prey as closely as she dares. She decides it is a worthwhile target. Instantly her huge body bursts into motion. She turns away, circles around and launches herself at the unsuspecting creature near the line of surf. She is travelling at full speed when she hits the 80-kilo prey – 17 times lighter than she is – with such incredible force that she drives it almost two metres out of the water.

Her jaws snap shut around the prey's body, she falls back into the water in a fountain of spray, thrashing and rolling about as she savages the life out of the creature she has caught. She is an awesomely efficient predator and the creature is dead within seconds. With virtually all of her energy now spent, the shark releases her prey and slowly cruises around it, resting, till she is ready to eat.

Later, a mangled surfboard washes ashore. There is no sign of its rider, and there never will be. The denizens of the shore weep and hunt for the murderer. Several sharks are caught and executed, but his killer is not one of them. She is patrolling elsewhere, looking for more prey.

She does not know that he had a name, a family and a promising business career, that he was a nice guy and would be sorely missed by his friends and relatives. She feels no remorse, because she is a predator, and no such thing is programmed into her. He was just something to eat at a time when she was hungry.

That is how and why a typical shark attack takes place. It will happen again, and it will continue happening for as long as there are surfers, divers and other humans using the oceans. We may be masters of the landmasses, but we have not conquered the sea, and it's likely that we never will. The 'Blue Continent', as someone once called it, belongs to the shark, a magnificent creature that is worthy of our attention ... and our respect, whenever we trespass into its domain.

ONE

A sharkaholic is born

It was June 1959, I was 11 years old and the sardine run around Amanzimtoti on the south coast of Natal (today's KwaZulu-Natal) had started with a vengeance. The yearly migration of massive shoals of these sought-after little fish always has an amazing effect on the population of this tranquil stretch of coast, and the 1959 run was no exception. Tradesmen downed tools and shop-owners closed up to join the rest of the community in their mad rush into the breakers to scoop up as much of the silvery harvest as they could.

From my vantage point on an outcrop of boulders near the water's edge I watched the grown-ups darting frenziedly about, pursuing the huge shoals of sardines with all sorts of implements. The general excitement soon got to me, and I began climbing down from the boulders to get a little closer to the action. I was nearly on the beach when a large wave came crashing in and deposited a massive shark on the sand, less than three metres from me.

To say that my 11-year-old mind had some difficulty comprehending what was happening before my eyes would be an all-time understatement. One moment I was excitedly scrambling down the rocks, the next I was confronted by a monster from the deep, which seemed to be at least twice my size and close enough to bite me in half.

I was seized with such terrible fear that I literally wet myself as I watched the shark thrashing about and baring its rows of shiny, hook-like teeth. Like most youngsters who had grown up on the Natal south coast I had been brought up on a heavy diet of shark horror stories and folklore, and all I wanted was to get as far away from it as quickly as possible. But the fear, mingled with a strange fascination, overwhelmed me so completely that I couldn't move a finger.

Then both the fascination and the fear were dispelled by a strange excitement that I had never felt before, and I found myself filled with an uncontrollable urge to capture or kill this fearsome enemy – right away. I shouted frantically at some people nearby who were also watching the sardine run, and headed for the shark.

Exactly how I would go about conquering it I didn't know; all I knew was that I had to get to grips with it ... now! One way or another, that massive shark was not going to get away from me. I was so completely gripped by the strange new excitement that I was completely oblivious to the danger I was in. All that saved me was a warning shout from one of the adults who had heard my piping war cries, so that I hesitated for a moment, and in that moment the next big wave came crashing in. When it receded, the shark was gone, pulled back into the sea.

I stood there in stunned disappointment, looking at the spot where the shark's mighty body had been churning up the sand only moments earlier, still shaken by that strange rush of exultation, and knew I would never forget it. I didn't realise, however, that I had reached a turning point in my life.

There is no monument to mark the place and moment of my epiphany, but even if South Africans were mad enough to indulge in such things it wouldn't be necessary, because only about two years later that very same rock ledge achieved ever-lasting notoriety when a swimmer was hauled out there, horribly mauled and bleeding to death – the first of five fatal shark-attack victims in just under three weeks in the Amanzimtoti area during the Christmas holiday.

The sharks' brief reign of terror, which has gone down in South African history as 'Black December', sparked general hysteria along the entire Natal coastline. There was a mass exodus by thousands of inland holiday-makers who had flocked to the sea for the traditional end-of-year frolics, and both locals and the remaining tourists refused point-blank to enter the water. (Three decades later, the paranoia is as strong as ever, and anti-shark nets have been erected at huge cost along more than 45 kilometres of the shoreline.) But by then I was already a seasoned shark hunter.

About 18 months after my encounter with the shark at Chain Rocks I watched an angler fighting a large shark from that same outcrop. As the battle raged, I was fascinated to see how the angler seemed to become one with the fish whose herculean efforts to escape were bending his rod like a bow.

It was a fight literally to the death, yet the thin nylon line locked them like an umbilical cord into a very personal relationship in which there was no room for anyone else. When he eventually landed the shark – it was about the same size as the one I first encountered – I had my first-ever opportunity for a really close and personal meeting. It was an unbelievable experience and without doubt was the catalyst that triggered my journey into the world of sharks.

My entry into the exciting and challenging world of the shark hunter was not easy. Firstly, I had none of the kit I would need, not even the most basic items, and no chance of getting it from my parents. The best description of my family would be 'poor and pretty damned unstable'. My dad was in the building trade, and all the money he earned was split between booze and domestic expenses like rent and food. So I became a crook.

It was a natural progression, because in my home being a bit dishonest was cause for praise rather than punishment. I forged raffle and Boy Scout 'bob-a-job' sheets, and before long I began to accumulate some funds for the basic necessities, a 12-foot blue marlin rod and a Penn 500 Jigmaster reel. It's not something I'm proud of today, having raised three children of my own, but that's how it happened. All I can say in mitigation is that I had had some doubtful values instilled in me, and that at least it was done in pursuit of a grand passion, not just because I wanted money to blow on ephemeral pleasures like sweets, soft drinks or cinema tickets.

In any case, I spent two weeks practising furiously with the fruits of my junior conman activities till I was able to cast my line out to about 60 metres. As far as I was concerned I was now ready to become a genuine card-carrying angler. But becoming a member of the rock-angling fraternity and its exciting activities wasn't easy by any means.

The veterans in the game guarded their favourite fishing spots jealously, and they didn't hesitate to invite me to bugger off (or worse) if they thought I was getting underfoot or trying to encroach on their territory. But I wasn't easily discouraged; my intermittently unhappy home life had toughened my spirit, and I've always been pretty much a glutton for punishment.

So I left the old salts to their favourite haunts and concentrated on the less popular spots, where no one cared about a skinny, obsessive kid with considerably less than ideal kit. My successes rarely exceeded my expectations. In two years of rock and surf fishing I landed only a handful of fish that weighed more than a kilogram apiece, and my biggest shark had great difficulty in pushing the scale past the four-kilo mark.

But it was not a wasted effort. I was out in the open air, I was gaining experience and I became addicted to fishing itself. It set a pattern that has persisted ever since. I am grateful just to be out there with rod and line; the fish I catch are a bonus.

As time passed I slowly worked my way into the fraternity to the point where I was allowed to become one of the regulars at the choice spots. And then, one day, my very short and hitherto unspectacular shark-hunting career took a swing for the better.

The great moment came one Sunday morning about six weeks after Alfie Maine, the self-appointed king of Chain Rocks, had allowed me to start fishing the deep channel off this famed outcrop of boulders. It was windless and the water was dead calm, and even at the tender age of 13 I knew instinctively that such conditions were very special, because anything could happen.

For some reason I have always tended to be gripped by haste and a sort-of desperation on the rare occasions when conditions are perfect, as they were on that particular day. The only explanation I have is that I become frightened that, if I don't hurry, the magic moment will pass before I can enjoy it to the full.

Anyway, the desperation had me in a firm grip that Sunday. I hurried to catch some small live bait, got it on my hook and half-ran to a rock ledge on Alfie Maine's left, where I cast as far out as my strength allowed. But the moment I sent my baited trace hurtling out I realised that I was in serious trouble.

In my haste I had not cast straight ahead, and my heart jumped into my throat when my sinker splashed into the water to the right of Alfie Maine's line. This was a serious blunder in the angler's world, which ran according to its own strict code of ethics; and my pathetic attempt to ignore this terrible faux pas in the hope that somehow things would sort themselves out was torpedoed almost immediately by an irate bellow from Alfie.

'Hey, arsehole, you've cast your line over mine! You do that again and I'll kick your sorry little arse into the sea!' It was like the Archangel Gabriel descending on me, and I started to retrieve my line amid a babble of apologies. But Alfie shouted: 'Leave your line where it is; dip your rod and I'll move to your left.' I obeyed, and soon our crossed lines were untangled again. I had learnt a valuable lesson in my education as an angler.

Less than five minutes later things got really exciting. Something very large and strong took my bait, nearly ripping the rod out of my hands and pulling the tip down at an alarming angle in spite of my puny best efforts. The pull was so strong that as I battled with hundreds of massive sharks and game fish, and became a trademark that is with me still.

Alfie must have sensed the change because he stopped shouting instructions and spent the last 40 minutes or so of my battle with the unknown fish calmly coaching me, tapping into the deep reservoir of experience he had built up over the years. He didn't raise his voice again till he saw the hooked fish just below the surface nearby. Then he bellowed: 'Oh, my fuck, look at that fucking monster you've got on your line!'

Moments later a ragged-tooth shark of monstrous size (well, maybe not by my later standards, but certainly then) that was at least as long as I was came to the surface only a couple of metres from where I was standing. It was unbelievable. I had caught this huge creature, me, Theo Ferreira, all of 13 years old! While Alfie and one of the other adults gaffed the shark, dragged its thrashing body onto the rocks and stabbed it to death, I let rip with the same profanities my unlikely mentor had bellowed a few moments earlier.

By now everybody in the vicinity was in an advanced state of excitement, which erupted into a frenzy when the shark pulled the needle of Alfie's fish scale to its 100-pound limit and would clearly have pulled it down even further. This set off a loud debate and an orgy of guesstimating, the upshot of which was consensus that the shark weighed more than 120 pounds. I found myself being congratulated and slapped on the back, a 13-year-old man among men, and some very special men at that.

Over the next three decades I would do battle with massive sharks that nightmares are made of. I would become a world-famous hunter of the great white shark. But I will never, ever, lose the flavour of that special day when I became a committed and almost obsessive sharkaholic.

After that there was no going back. By the time I was 14 I had saved enough money by doing odd jobs to buy a rod that was capable of handling the large customers, and during the following three years my fishing skills developed to the point where I was doing regular battle with sharks and rays from the piers along the Durban waterfront.

By the time I was 18 I had acquired a couple of other interests – girls and motorbikes, to be specific – which provided the sharks with some strong competition, but never quite made it to first place in my affections ... with one exception, a fetching girl named Norma Shirley Netcher. We clicked right away – if ever there was a love-match made in heaven, this was it.

Norma had no interest in fishing, but she was willing to spend many hours in all kinds of weather to be with me while I did battle off the rocks, and I grew to love and respect her so much that when we discovered that she was pregnant (with Craig, although of course we didn't know that yet in those pre-ultrasound days), marrying her was a privilege rather than a societal obligation.

Once we had broken the news to our respective parents we didn't let the grass grow under our feet. A few weeks later we were married by a local magistrate and then went off to her parents' home for a rather raucous reception featuring lots of booze and interaction, which sometimes turned a little aggressive – one way and another, a reception no one was likely to forget in a hurry.

My sister Cathy, who lived in the coastal town of Empangeni, about two hours by rail from Durban, insisted that we spend our honeymoon with her and her husband, Andries. This suited us fine, so we left the reception to take care of itself and went off to catch a train. Late that afternoon we arrived at Empangeni, where Andries and Cathy were waiting to pick us up.

We had barely carried our bags into their home when our brand-new marriage was put to its first test. Andries informed me that the cob were running at the mouth of Richards Bay lagoon and needed thinning out, and within minutes it was agreed that he and I would go off to assist in the process.

This evoked strong protests from Cathy, who stated that this was no suitable activity for my honeymoon night. Being quite familiar with the peculiar workings of an angler's mind, she did not place any faith in our promises to be back no later than half-past eight.

We were not to be denied, however, and in due course arrived at the lagoon. A number of other anglers were there already, and within a few minutes we had our lines in the water and were chatting to some nice-sized fish. Then (as Cathy had anticipated) we lost track of time and our two-hour stint stretched on into the early hours. We finally got back around two o'clock in the morning and were pounced on by Cathy, who gave us (and me in particular) a thorough bollocking. When I finally managed to escape to our bedroom I was confronted by a very unhappy and tearful wife.

It was all pretty traumatic. I was still young and not fully house-trained, and I hadn't quite worked out why the women in my life found it so hard to understand that, while they were always there, the fish came on the bite without warning, and if you were not available at that precise moment the opportunity was lost.

I'm glad to say, though, that our marriage survived this stern test, and there wasn't another one till Norma went into labour one afternoon seven months later. I rushed her off to hospital, and by four o'clock she was booked in and bedded, and I was allowed in to see her. No doubt I looked a little distracted, as fathers-to-be tend to look, but neither Norma nor the others realised that in addition to my worry that something might go wrong with the birth, the skipjack – fine fighting fish – had been feeding well at 'T' jetty in the harbour, and late afternoon was the best time to do business with them.

So, callous swine that I was, I convinced Norma that she needed to try to relax and get some sleep, and said I would be back in a little while. Then I slipped away to the harbour, rod in hand. By the time I returned about four hours later, contented with my afternoon's angling and smelling a bit fishy, Craig was already almost two hours old. I had no idea at the time of how much my thoughtless selfishness must have hurt the very special and gentle creature I had married, and I hope that I somehow managed to make this up to her over the next 30 years before she was taken from me.

I had now reached such a level of piscatorial skill that I was landing up to 12 sharks a night. My obsession with hunting sharks was so intense that the other regulars on the piers took to calling me 'Sharky'. The holiday-makers who frequented the beachfront all the year round constantly bombarded me with questions about my exploits and often wanted to be photographed with me and the sharks that I had killed. It all went to my head, of course, and before long I was seeing myself as a hero, a sort of latter-day slayer of dragons whose mission was to rid the world of the man-eating monsters of the sea.

Well, a dragon-slayer I wasn't, since not one of the sharks that I slaughtered over this period could have been considered a threat to humans. And I didn't realise what a small-time operator I really was. At this early stage of my career I reckoned a large shark was one that was about two and a half metres long with a weight of about 180 kilos. What I still had to discover was that each of the 'large' sharks I was pulling out of the water would be little more than a tasty snack to the giants of the deep that I would encounter later on.

But all that would come as I travelled further down the road of my obsessive involvement with predator sharks.

TWO

Great white shark hunter: the early days ... and I prepare to meet the 'Submarine'

As I grew to manhood in the early 1970s my shark-hunting activities progressed from land to sea when I became a deckhand on fishing trawlers, and before long I was landing large dusky bull and other predator sharks. But the owners and skippers of the various boats did not share my obsession. They were only interested in catching edible fish which they could sell.

This was a reasonable enough attitude, since they had bills to pay and sharks didn't bring in much money. But for an obsessed sharkaholic like myself it was a serious obstacle, and I found it very difficult to be just a regular crew member. As a result I was always in trouble with one tight-arsed skipper or another, and eventually it became clear that the only way to get shot of these problems would be to get my own boat and hunt sharks when I felt like it.

By 1977 I was ready to take the plunge, a serious one for a married man with kids. Throwing caution to the wind, I bought my first deep-sea fishing boat, and within six weeks I had chucked my job, sold the furniture, packed my family's bags and moved down to the Cape of Good Hope to make (I hoped) a handsome living catching snoek, that wonderful oily fish that abounds around the southern tip of the continent.

The possibility of running into some of the great white sharks that were said to roam the Cape waters was an added inducement to move south. I would rather have died than admit it, but

I suffered from a fairly substantial dose of the *Jaws* mentality at that time.

How much of the great whites' alleged abundance was fact and how much legend was not quite clear. For example, there was the story of the great white known as the 'Submarine' which was instantly identifiable by a missing piece of dorsal fin shaped like a half-moon. It was between seven and ten metres long – the actual size depended on who was telling the story and how many shots of rum or brandy he'd wet his whistle with – and weighed anything up to a couple of thousand kilos.

The Submarine, so it was said, attacked ski boats and small yachts without provocation, and if you hooked it, it was likely to rip the line's cleats clean off the boat and bend open the largest, toughest custom-made hooks. And so on and so on, each tale more hair-raising than the next. It was said that someone had placed a reward of R2 000 (a not inconsiderable sum of money at the time) on its unrepentant head.

What sharkaholic could resist such tales, especially when he hung on to every slurred word of the story? These characters were preservers of the myth we all wanted to believe. Being a cocky type, I often had sarcastic questions and comments about the authenticity of these tales; I had become arrogant enough to consider myself to be the big-shot shark hunter who had come face to face with some of the really large sharks.

At that early stage of my career a really big shark was about three metres long and weighed in at around 200 to 300 kilos. Now these idiot storytellers wanted me to believe that this so-called Submarine was about three times that size and weighed in at around ten times as much! My favourite put-down was: 'You guys have obviously been watching a Moby Dick movie.'

Little did I know that, in the not-too-distant future, I would not only come face to face with this nightmare from the deep but that this hair-raising first encounter would also have such a profound effect on me that it would affect my entire future.

Well, I didn't meet up with the Submarine right away, but the great white sharks proved to be there, all right, and my first face-to-face encounter with one of these mighty creatures took me down a couple of pegs. The meeting took place while my 12-year-old son Craig and I were on a weekend fishing trip in False Bay. As it happened the pickings were poor, and Craig became bored. I was bored, too, and when he asked if he could use the old tuna rod and reel on the boat to try to catch a shark, I was quite amenable.

Craig attached a tuna trace and hook to the line, baited the hook with a large squid-head and tossed it into the water at the stern. I went back to being bored, but the line had not been in the water for more than five minutes when he shouted that he had hooked something big and that he couldn't hold on to it. Unconsciously echoing Alfie Maine's words of so many years ago, I replied to Craig: 'You hooked the sucker, so you'd better land it, sonny.'

It was soon evident that Craig had hooked into something really big, possibly too big for a little chap who only weighed 42 kilos soaking wet, but he hung on with a grim determination that reminded me of myself on the unforgettable day of the ragged-tooth shark. Everyone on board shouted advice and encouragement to him in his battle with the creature at the end of his line, but the struggle was so fierce that at times he would cry out from the pain and strain he was enduring.

Eventually, however, he managed to bring his catch in to the boat. The moment I laid my eyes on the exhausted creature wallowing in the water close to the boat, I knew without doubt that at last I had come face to face with a genuine great white shark. I had watched *Jaws* many times, and there was no mistaking the large triangular teeth and the broad big-gilled head with its staring golf ball-sized black eyes. The unmistakable dorsal fin was the final piece of magic that rounded off this stunning picture.

As I feasted my eyes on that magnificent shark, it suddenly dawned on me that my 12-year-old son had hooked and brought in – all by himself – by far the biggest shark that I had ever laid eyes on. My slap of congratulations on Craig's back was so hard that the bugger almost ended up in the water with the shark.

It was too large to load on board, so we tied a rope to the tail and towed it back to Gordon's Bay harbour. It weighed 293 kilos, over 80 kilos more than biggest shark I had caught so far, and my deep-rooted passion for hunting the sea predators became inflamed almost to the point of spontaneous combustion.

Over the next three and a half years I hooked and fought at least 60 white sharks, and landed 28 of them. The largest was one hell of a shark in any man's language. All of 4.8 metres long, with a maximum girth of 3.4 metres, it tipped the scale at 1 248 kilos, and for sheer power and stubbornness far outclassed all the others. It still remains one of the crowning glories of my white shark hunting career.

In the same week that Craig hooked and landed his first white shark, I started shopping around for equipment suitable for fighting and landing the giant predators. It took me a few days to acquire all the tackle that I needed, and then I set about making my first terminal white shark trace.

This 'mother of all traces' consisted of the largest tuna hook on the market, attached to an eight-metre length of 250-kilo steel cable and a ten-litre plastic drum. Satisfied that this was the meanest white shark trace around, I proudly showed it off to my friends and crew, and wasn't shy about boasting that it would sort out the meanest white shark the ocean could throw at me.

Two weeks later I had the opportunity to put my bold claims to the test. Armed with my heavy big-game fishing rod, the special terminal trace and 50 litres of ox blood mixed with mashed sardines, my crew and I left Gordon's Bay harbour in the early hours of the morning and headed out for the Macassar Beach area in search of a great white.

When we had anchored some 800 metres off the beach I baited my special trace's hook with a large red roman I had just caught and told Craig to start chumming. The chum soon formed a shiny crimson slick, spreading like an oily red ribbon over the calm ocean.

As I sat there in the swivel chair in my old leather shoulder fighting harness, my anticipation of the moment when a white shark would arrive surged every time the buoy bobbed on the surface as the red roman attached to it tried to swim away, my pulse quickening and a wave of excitement welling up inside me. I was as certain as I was of the sun rising the next morning that I was going to come face to face with a great white that day and do battle with it, although I could not have explained why.

Before long, this became a reality. The sun was making its lazy way across the sky towards noon when the water about ten metres behind the buoy suddenly came to life with a large whirl-pool-like surface action. Moments later a massive great white shark glided into view some three metres from the stern.

Although my eyes took in what they were seeing, my mind had difficulty in coping with this real-life *Jaws* drama unfolding before me. The head was at least three times bigger than any other I had ever seen. The jet-black eye staring at me seemed larger than a tennis ball. Its slightly gaping jaw showed rows of shiny, razor-sharp teeth, as if giving me a menacing warning. Behind the head was a shiny muscular body of at least four and a half metres long, and I realised this monster from the deep must weigh close to a ton.

As the creature's massive proportions began to sink in, I suddenly became aware of how very small and vulnerable my 5.6-metre boat was in comparison with the shark as it casually closed the gap between us to less than two metres, unaware of the effect it was having on everyone on board. It was a totally new ballgame, and I found myself confronted with a frightening new challenge that at that moment scared me shitless. My only consolation was that I saw the others huddling close together – at least I wasn't the only one to be frightened.

Intent on its task, the shark turned and homed in on the red roman attached to the buoy. The bait-fish made a desperate effort to dodge, then disappeared into the shark's gaping mouth like a tasty finger snack and was swallowed in one smooth motion. The shark glided past the stern of the boat, the shiny steel trace trailing behind it.

I knew what was happening. Instead of sliding smoothly down the shark's throat to the acid digestive fluids in its stomach, the tasty morsel was about to come to an abrupt halt as the needle-sharp hook started biting into flesh.

Moments later the shark realised that there was something seriously wrong as its forward movement exerted increasing pressure on the hook and drove it deeply into the walls of the creature's throat. Instantly the shark's gentle dive turned into a desperate panic-stricken rush as it tried to escape. But at that moment the slack was taken up on the steel trace-wire, and the resistance of the ten-litre plastic drum arrested the shark's forward rush, driving the hook even deeper into its flesh. The new wave of pain drove the shark into a blind panic and the buoy ripped along the surface behind it as it tried desperately to escape from this unexpected and unknown danger.

My crew and I watched in a state of hypnotised silence. Our minds were still trying to kick into gear when the buoy suddenly disappeared below the surface in a plume of spray and the ratchet on the big-game fishing reel screamed as the line was stripped from it. That broke the spell, and I could hear my voice shouting instructions to my crew as I manoeuvred myself quickly onto the fish hatch and hooked the rod up to the harness.

The 1 200 metres of line on the reel was being stripped off far too rapidly; I allowed the line to run out for a further five seconds, then threw the clutch on the reel and slammed back with the full weight of my 120-kilo frame. The force that the hooked shark exerted against my harness was incredible. Never in my wildest dreams had I ever imagined that any shark was capable of such raw power and determined resistance. Within five minutes of commencing this fierce battle a steady stream of perspiration stung my eyes and blurred my vision as it ran down my face, and I could feel the muscles in my shoulders and back knotting up.

The battle between us raged for about 15 minutes, and then the line suddenly went slack. The shark had got away! As I reeled in the slack line I struggled to get my mind to accept that the shark could have torn loose from the large hook that I had witnessed disappearing down its throat a while earlier. I was even less inclined to accept that either the ultraheavy-duty trace or the line could have failed. *What the hell had gone wrong? How could this bastard fish have come loose?*

When the trace was finally reeled in we couldn't believe our eyes. About a metre above the hook this monster of a great white had bitten clean through the 250-kilo steel wire in which I had had so much confidence. As we inspected it, voicing our sheer disbelief, I realised that I had totally underestimated the incredible power and fighting ability of the giant predators.

Over the next seven weeks I suffered much frustration and received a supersized dent in my ego as no fewer than five sharks were lost in mid-battle as a result of equipment failure. But, being an obstinate glutton for punishment, I didn't give up and eventually I designed a white shark terminal rig of such overkill proportions that I reckoned the odds had swung strongly into my favour.

I had upgraded the steel trace to an eight-metre length of winch cable with a breaking strain of 1 000 kilos and paired it with a 25-litre drum. I reckoned the cable would certainly be a match for even the most formidable white shark jaw, and the 25-litre drum would cause enough drag to completely exhaust any shark, even if the 60-kilo fishing line broke.

My new equipment heightened my anticipation to such a level that I couldn't wait to resume battle. Now, I was confident, the white sharks I hooked would almost certainly be doomed to die the moment they swallowed the bait; there was no way that these stubborn fighting machines were going to be able to escape when my oversized razor-sharp hook took hold of them.

Now I was ready for anything, and I looked forward with keen anticipation to resuming my one-man war with the great whites … perhaps even with the legendary Submarine about which I had heard such lurid tales back on the Natal coast.

THREE

Theo and the Submarine: living the Jaws *nightmare*

'Face to face with your worst possible nightmare' is a mild way of describing my first encounter with the notorious Submarine. My date with this monster from the deep came up when we were anchored about a kilometre off Macassar Beach on one of our regular weekend fishing trips.

Craig was playing a five-kilo pyjama shark that he had hooked, and since the bottom fish were biting well I warned him that if he allowed his shark to tangle with my lines, he would be thrown overboard to join it. Craig decided not to put this threat to the test and moved clear of the space I had taken over for myself. Shades of Alfie Maine and the 13-year-old stripling called Theo Ferreira all those years ago.

I was baiting up my hook again after landing a fair-sized red roman when Craig shouted from behind me: 'Dad, Dad, there's a giant shark under the boat!' Knowing him to be a pretty cool character, I had no doubt that he had seen something pretty dramatic, and from the shock and emotion in his voice I could tell that whatever it was had scared the hell out of him.

I dropped what I was doing and spun around to face him, and when I saw the flushed, wild-eyed look on his face a shiver raced through my body; it was impossible not to feel and react to his excitement; clearly he had seen something totally awesome. As quickly as I could, I joined him where he was peering over the side. What could have caused such an electric reaction?

Then I saw what he was looking at, and my blood seemed to turn to ice. 'Oh shit, we're in big trouble!' I heard myself blurt out. 'This fucker is going to wipe the boat out!' My heart began pumping at twice its normal rate and my mind raced out of control as I found myself looking into a cruel, shiny black pit of an eye, set into an enormous shark head that was certainly the broadest I had ever seen; the seemingly endless body with its gigantic dorsal and pectoral fins brought back nightmare scenes from the *Jaws* movies.

Except that there was obviously one big difference. This was no make-believe terror tale we were watching in the safety of a cinema. This was the real thing, and it was pretty damn scary. So scary that it felt almost unreal to know that I was fully conscious and wide awake, on an open boat a mere 5.7 metres long that was dwarfed by this mother of all sharks – which, to make matters worse, was less than two metres away.

The boil of emotion and fear that gripped me at that moment is as vivid now as it was then. I was certain that at last I had met the legendary Submarine. She had to be one of the largest great whites ever to be encountered by humankind, and here I was, eyeballing her at close quarters.

With absolute confidence the Submarine slowly cruised to the surface next to the boat. As if drawn by a magnet, Craig scrambled along the deck towards the bow, following the incredible creature's progress. When he had got as far as he could go, he shouted: 'The shark's head is at the front of the boat. It's massive, Dad!'

I looked back and saw that her tail was still at least a metre short of reaching the stern, and I knew that we had found the Submarine even before I spotted the plate-sized arc missing from the dorsal fin, the large light blotches on her back and the battle-scarred snout and head. All the outrageous stories that I'd scoffed at rushed back to me, and I realised that, for once, the exaggerations hadn't been exaggerations after all.

The giant shark turned gracefully at the bow and came gliding back. Now the visual impact was even more overwhelming and made our little boat look punier and more vulnerable than ever before. Imagine a heavyweight wrestler taking on a child weighing 40 kilos, and you will have some idea of our predicament. Huge though it was, her head seemed small and out of proportion to her massive body, which from the tip of one pectoral fin to the other was at least a metre wider than the boat's total 1.8-metre width.

If this shark were to lie on the beach, the highest point of her back would be about level with the bellybutton of a tall man, and the tip of her dorsal fin at eye-level. I imagined the Submarine being loaded onto a short-wheelbase railway truck, and knew that between her body and pectoral fins she would most certainly be too wide to fit.

Now the potential danger of the situation started sinking in, and I became very aware of the fact that this incredible creature swimming so close to us could easily turn the nightmare stories I had heard into ghastly reality. No wonder she managed to scare fishermen shitless.

This realisation triggered an adrenaline rush that dispelled the paralysing terror and shocked my brain back into gear. An uncontrollable urge to kill the monster gripped me, the same urge that had been lit in me 20 years earlier at Amanzimtoti, and I cursed the fact that today of all days I had decided to target bottom fish and left all my shark-hunting equipment at home.

I scrambled around, trying to find something to do battle with. The fish gaff was the only item remotely capable of hooking the Submarine. Hands shaking, I started tying some anchor rope on its cane handle, shouting to Craig to pass me a large red roman with which to bait the hook.

Craig started to respond, then stopped and looked me in the eyes with what I can only describe as respectful defiance. 'Dad,' he said, 'there's no way that you can fight that shark with the equipment you're trying to put together.' I looked down at the gaff and anchor-line in my trembling fingers and realised how crazy I must look to the others. A sheepish grin crept over my face, and the whole crew exchanged glances and then burst into uncontrollable laughter that was fuelled by shock, fear and other mixed emotions.

While we laughed like lunatics the Submarine slowly circled the boat in what appeared to be a very purposeful manner, looking at us with her emotionless black eyes, her immense jaw showing the rows of razor-sharp teeth. I stared back at the stunning creature and thought to myself: *You're mine, you arrogant bitch. I'll be back to nail you.*

Then she thrashed her powerful tail before gracefully disappearing from the surface and sight, as abruptly as she had made her dramatic appearance.

As my adrenaline level slowly began to subside I became aware that a very dramatic change had come over me in the short space of time that the Submarine had been alongside. For reasons that I found impossible to explain, then or even many years later, I had developed an uncontrollable obsession to hunt her down, to challenge her might and kill her.

For the following three years I would be consumed by this obsession. I would find it impossible to discard, and I would launch a one-sided war with the Submarine that would develop into a bitter personal vendetta. It took such control of my life that I spent most of my time dreaming about hunting and destroying the Submarine. I was so strongly focused that I actually began to regard her as my personal prey, and God help anyone who was stupid enough to get in my way.

Over the two-year period after my move to the shores of the Cape I operated in the False Bay area, and enjoyed a high level of success at hunting great whites. This resulted in regular media reports on my escapades, and the resulting high profile soon generated interest from potential sponsors.

One of these was a large inland waterproofing company whose managing director was keen to get exposure by linking the company logo and name to my shark-hunting activities. After a few telephone conversations we arranged that he would fly down from Johannesburg and meet up with me at Gordon's Bay, and then I would take him out on a hunt so that he could evaluate the situation first hand.

In due course he arrived in Cape Town and drove out to Gordon's Bay where he joined us – my regular crewman, Trevor Grant, and myself, plus Craig and his friend Devon, who were on their school holidays. We left the harbour at first light the next morning, covered the 12 sea miles to the Macassar Beach area within 20 minutes and found a nice pinnacle of reef on the echo sounder, where we anchored. Soon we had some lines in the water to catch a fish for bait, and I told Trevor to start ladling out our chum of ox blood and mashed pilchards.

Craig, our shark-bait king, soon landed a fair-sized spotted gully shark, which I rigged up to the terminal trace. This was old hat to me, but to impress my potential benefactor I made a bit of an extra show of embedding the custom-made hook into the flesh at the base of the shark's dorsal fin. This done, I dropped the gully shark into the water, and as it strained against the rig I fed the 800-kilo breaking-strain steel cable in after it till the plastic drum splashed into the water next to the boat.

Craig and Devon had taken over chumming duties in the meantime and soon had a steady flow trickling over the side. The slick slowly drifted downstream from the boat. For some reason the sight of an oily red streak in the water always seemed to complete the setting of a white shark hunt for me.

Before long the plastic drum, which had been bobbing gently from the gully shark's attempts to escape, exploded from the surface in an impressive plume of water and foam that was flecked with crimson droplets of diluted ox blood and glowed as the morning sun reflected off it. A white shark had arrived! It couldn't have been a more spectacular display for my guest and potential sponsor if I had personally orchestrated it for maximum effect.

As if that was not dramatic enough, the ratchet on my rod's big reel started screeching like a band saw as the line was ripped off it. What a perfect start! I dived into the fighting chair, grabbed the rod from its holder and snapped the straps of the fighting harness onto the reel. Let battle commence.

I allowed the screaming reel to peel off line for another five seconds before slamming the clutch tight. The line snapped to an abrupt halt as I leaned my full weight back against the rod. The pressure exerted by this fleeing shark was incredible. Never had I imagined that any shark could deliver such an intense show of raw power, and I realised that I was going to have my hands full with this one.

The line was peeling off the spool far too quickly. *Oh, shit,* I thought, *if I don't stop this baby, I am going to lose it.* Urgently I shouted orders to up-anchor and fire up the outboard motors so we could follow the shark, but more than 1 000 metres of the 1 200 metres on the reel had gone by the time that Craig had started up and set off after our prey.

Even with the boat following the fleeing shark at a fast trawling pace it was exerting incredible pressure on the harness, so that for the first time in my shark-hunting career I experienced the feeling of having my head forced down between my legs and up my backside ... not a happy place from which to view the world. This was the result of the continuous down-and-forward pressure being applied by the stubborn bugger that had taken our hook.

I summoned up all the determination I could muster and got down to showing the shark exactly who was in charge. The shark obviously wasn't paying attention, though, and for the next hour and a half the plastic drum never once popped to the surface. It really staggered me that the shark could do this while simultaneously laying such massive pressure on me and my rod, to which I was clinging for dear life.

Eventually the strain started taking a serious physical toll of my endurance, and what had started out as an exciting challenge became a grim do-or-die battle with this amazingly strong sea beast, which none of us had laid eyes on so far, in spite of the fact that I was getting a heavy-duty clobbering that I would never forget. Surprisingly, it had not yet dawned on anybody, even at that late stage, that I might be hooked to the Submarine.

My potential sponsor had been very quiet and unobtrusive up to this point, but now he relaxed and started warming to the excitement and drama of the battle, so much so that he became positively chirpy and started wisecracking about how 'we' were going to sort the shark out. I listened and allowed myself a discreet smile. Little did this guy know that his eyes were going to pop and that he would be gripped by a large dose of fear when he came face to face with what I had on the end of my line.

The plastic drum suddenly jumped to the surface some 200 metres from the boat, followed a few moments later by the shark's dorsal and tail fins a few metres from it. Although we were some distance from it, the familiar adrenaline rush started pumping when I saw the unmistakable half-moon gap in the dorsal fin and realised that I had hooked the Submarine.

Son-of-a-bitch! I've got you, you bastard, I've got you! I exulted silently when this sank in. I instructed Craig to get closer to the shark and then told the others about what we were contending with. Abruptly the festive mood was replaced by a ghastly silence.

Craig rapidly closed the gap till we were within 20 metres of the mammoth creature, and from my vantage point I noticed that she was wallowing near the surface of the water in what seemed to be total exhaustion. At the sight of my old adversary lying so close in the water I abandoned the cautious approach I always used when handling large, strong sharks and told Craig to get as close to the Submarine's tail as possible, so that we could drop a tow-rope around it. Once that was done we could tow her back to Gordon's Bay.

That was the first mistake. The second came when Craig, who was as excited as I was, blipped the throttle a little too hard and the boat surged directly at the shark. The Submarine became aware of the boat bearing down on her and suddenly came back to life, slashing about with her oversized tail and then heading straight for us.

Just to add to the shit that was about to hit the fan, I made one more major mistake in those critical seconds. Lacking confidence in Craig's ability to outmanoeuvre the shark, I shoved him aside and grabbed the helm and throttles so that I could power the boat out of the shark's way. Those critical seconds between shoving Craig aside and taking the controls made the difference between escaping the oncoming Submarine and the disaster that was to follow.

Moments later the shit finally hit the fan in a big way. A cold fist seemed to grab at my heart as I saw the Submarine dive under the boat. Immediately I swung the boat around in a desperate effort to avoid a collision, while my instincts screamed a warning that we were in big trouble. And we were.

The port motor jerked violently, followed moments later by the starboard one. The boat came to an abrupt halt, and I knew that our serious problem had become positively deadly; the looks of growing fear on the others' faces as they stared at me in deathly silence told me that they knew it as well.

I shook off my temporarily mesmerised state and turned the key to restart the motors. All I got was a metallic click that meant a jam, and I felt my stomach knotting up. I was still registering this when I heard my potential sponsor's quavering voice: 'Oh, shit, we're going to die, we're going to die!'

I turned my head to see what had caused this outburst and was gripped by raw panic myself. Less than three metres behind the motors the Submarine lay on the surface in all her terrifying glory, dwarfing our craft so completely that I felt like screaming and crying simultaneously. My first impressions of her had been correct: her head was almost as wide as the entire stern of the boat, and her pectoral fins each protruded for at least a metre from either side. I felt sick in the stomach. This time, I realised, I had bitten off one hell of a lot more than I could chew.

But the Submarine didn't give me much time to stand there feeling sorry for myself. She started whipping her body from side to side, and the boat did likewise. That confirmed my worst fears: the nine metres of steel cable, attached to the hook that was obviously still deeply embedded somewhere inside this very angry creature, had become firmly entangled in the propellers. This meant that the 900-kilo boat was attached to a 3 000-kilo sea monster by an umbilical cord with a breaking-strain of 1 000 kilos. All of which was most certainly a recipe for big, big trouble.

Fighting down the temptation to fall into a state of blind panic, I wrestled my emotions till I had them under full control again and began to focus on our immediate predicament. The first thing to do was scramble to the stern to assess our situation and see what could be done about it. What I saw when I got there was so bad that I heard myself saying out loud: 'Oh, my God, this is very bad, we're in big, big shit!' It was no more than the truth. The steel cable was jammed so tightly into the props that the piece between the two motors was pulled as taut as piano wire.

I paused, my mind racing as I tried to figure out a solution. But the Submarine didn't allow me any time to think, and all hell broke loose. Full of pain and aggression towards the strange object that was the cause of her woes, she gave two slashes of her massive tail and slammed into the stern with such a bone-jarring impact that I almost lost my footing and joined her in the water. Before any of us could recover she did it again, after which she grabbed the port motor in her cavernous mouth and started shaking the entire boat around like a rag doll.

This seemed to go on for a long, long time before she let go and sank back to her original position again, wallowing gently in the water as if her violent efforts had finally exhausted her. But scant moments later she slowly rolled onto her side and started slashing her tail with a wide sweeping motion, smoothly dipped her imposing head and went into a dive. The cable snapped taut with a jerk, and then the stern started bobbing around like a cork as the Submarine's massive body dipped to a 40-degree angle and started to gain momentum, her violently thrashing tail and fins finding purchase.

My heart popped into my throat as the taut cable began to pull the boat's transom lower and lower. Suffering shit! I couldn't believe what I was seeing. But the impossible was happening, all right. I don't know if it is possible for anyone reading this to imagine the raw horror we felt as we watched the stern sink lower and lower in the water till it actually started disappearing below the surface. Water cascaded onto the deck till it was sloshing over my feet while I looked down at it, unable to move. It was a real-life nightmare, far worse than anything Steven Spielberg in his wildest dreams could have thought up for any of his shark movies.

And there was no end to it in sight. The Submarine continued to dive, pulling the stern even deeper till only the top half of the engine covers were showing and the deck was tilted up at an angle of about 20 degrees, so that I was up to my calves in the water pouring over the transom.

Probably no more than about 30 seconds had passed since the Submarine had started diving, but everything seemed to be happening in slow motion. The strange thing was that in spite of the absolutely critical situation and my renewed panic I was acutely aware of every detail around me as I tried to find a way out of our desperate situation.

My potential sponsor had completely lost his composure and was cowering in the bow in a state of complete shock and terror, saying over and over: 'Oh, my God, are we in trouble, God, please save us!' Devon, poor little bugger, his eyes full of tears, kept saying: 'Craig, we're going to die, we're going to die!' But to my surprise I saw that Craig, on the other hand, had stayed comparatively calm and was actually trying to find something with which to cut the cable.

Then the Submarine let us pull back from the brink of disaster. Seemingly exhausted once more by her failure to dive away, she suddenly popped up again and returned to her original position. I seized the opportunity to scramble to the motors and start lifting one of them out of the water so that I could try to untangle the steel cable from the propeller.

Keeping one eye on the Submarine, I forced my shaking hands to start uncoiling the first loop of wire from the prop, but before I could accomplish anything, she returned to attack the boat again. I dived to safety (relatively speaking) as she crashed into the stern, grabbed the motor I had been working on and started jerking the boat from side to side again with such force that I could clearly hear metal creak and groan. Then she let go of the motor and started rolling against the stern and side of the boat, inflicting a succession of sledgehammer blows on the vessel.

Up to now the thought that she would attack and kill us had never entered my mind. I knew without even thinking about it that she was almost certainly as terrified as we were and was only intent on breaking free or destroying the thing that was tormenting her; yes, she could end up inflicting very serious damage, but somehow I didn't think that she would actually sink my boat. But as her frenzied efforts intensified I knew that my boat was taking a hell of a pounding and that all of us on board would be in very real danger if her desperate escape efforts were not cut short very soon.

My concern was not so much that the boat would sink; the real danger was that the Submarine was thrashing and rolling so violently that she might end up in the boat, and I remembered an incident of a few years earlier in which a white shark had jumped into a boat and caused damage and serious injury. This motivated me to get my arse into action, and I hurried to the radio to send out my first-ever Mayday call. A fishing boat anchored approximately a kilometre away responded, and rushed to the scene once I had informed the skipper of the boat about our desperate situation.

Our very welcome rescuers arrived on the scene within five minutes of the call, Craig jumping into the bow to toss a line to them. If we hadn't been fighting for our lives the looks of absolute shock on their faces would have been comical. They hung over the side with their jaws literally falling open as they watched the Submarine smashing against our boat while Craig shouted, rather unnecessarily: 'It's bigger than the boat, it's bigger than the boat!'

I asked them to tow us towards Gordon's Bay at about five knots, because I knew that anything faster might result in one of the motors being ripped off by the Submarine's drag and weight. I feared the worst, but once the two craft had picked up momentum the Submarine gave up bashing us, surfaced and allowed herself to be towed in the direction of Gordon's Bay; the raging monster had turned into a tame pussycat.

After we had covered about one sea mile I gradually began to relax, since the Submarine was being towed in a controlled manner and did not seem to pose any further threat to the boat or us. Slowly we started regaining our composure as we neared Gordon's Bay and the Submarine continued to behave herself, an almost hysterical carnival atmosphere taking the place of the nervous silence in which we had started the trip home. I looked back at this trophy of all trophies, puffing up with pride at my achievement in bagging such a fabled creature.

But suddenly the pride and exuberance left me, to be replaced by the urgent ringing of mental alarm bells. There was a serious problem coming up! The Submarine was being towed at a gentle speed, *headfirst instead of the other way around!* This meant that a constant flow of water was running over her gills, and feeding her fresh oxygen that was bound to revitalise her. And once the Submarine revived she would be most unlikely to roll over and play dead. What was more likely was that she would become an uncontrollable bundle of lethal energy just as we arrived at the harbour.

There was only one thing to do: increase the flow of water through the Submarine's mouth, which might be enough to flood her stomach and drown her. I raised the skipper of the fishing boat and asked him to gently increase his speed to about ten knots. He did so and we carried on without any reaction from the Submarine, and once more I began to feel more confident as we drew closer to Gordon's Bay.

But after just two kilometres or so the two boats were suddenly jerked almost to a standstill, so violently that if I had not known that the average depth below our keels was 12 fathoms I would have sworn we had hit a sandbar. Then a second later both surged forward with such force that we were all nearly knocked off our feet. I knew immediately what had happened, and spun around towards the stern with a sinking feeling in my heart. One quick look told me my suspicions were justified: my magnificent catch had disappeared.

To say I was bitterly disappointed would be putting it mildly; I felt as if a mule had kicked me in the guts as I went back to the stern and hauled the trace on board. We gaped in disbelief as we saw how the Submarine had made her escape. The massive hook, so strong that it could easily lift a V8 Detroit diesel engine weighing more than a ton, was bent wide open. The feat was almost beyond the realms of imagination. She had lain low, letting the flow of oxygen recharge her batteries, and when she was good and ready she had resisted the tow with such force that the hook had given way and slipped out of her flesh.

When we got to Gordon's Bay we pulled the boat up the slipway and onto its trailer so that we could inspect the damage. The portside motor had been twisted off-centre by about 20 degrees, both motors had deep tooth scars and the hull had a 30-centimetre crack in it. I simply shook my head as I stood there and assessed all this. The Submarine had definitely won this round. But it was only the first battle of what would become a full-on war.

FOUR

Live bait and the Sub

About 14 months after my second hair-raising encounter with the Submarine, a friend, named Arthur Ridgeway, from Strand near Gordon's Bay, who had been a big help in my hunting quest, asked if I could give him a white shark's jaw. I responded, 'Pal, if you want a jaw, you will have to get off your lazy backside and go to sea with me and help to land a white shark.'

Art was happy with this, and three days later we set off from Gordon's Bay towards a place where I had had good luck in finding white sharks, a reef about two kilometres off Macassar Beach. While he got a line in the water to catch some bait I prepared my 'terminal rig', as shark hunters call this type of device – in this case an enormous custom-made hook with an eight-metre steel trace and the usual plastic drum buoy.

Art soon hooked a grey shark weighing about 20 kilos. I embedded the hook in its back just below the dorsal fin, then dropped it overboard and fed out the trace as the shark moved away from the boat, attaching the plastic drum as the slack was taken up. This done, I checked my equipment. I was using a 60-kilo class Fenwick big-game rod with a Penn Senator 14\0 big-game reel loaded with 1 200 metres of 60-kilo Dacron line. Satisfied that everything was ready, I set the drag on the reel just tight enough to keep the bait-shark in check as it tugged at the bobbing plastic drum.

The arrival of a white shark at a bait is always a spectacular sight, and on this day it was no different. An enormous surface-action swirl suddenly appeared on the calm water about ten metres behind the drum, which started jigging violently up and down as the bait-shark realised that it was in big trouble. Seconds later the sleek grey torpedo shape of a four-metre white shark came cruising past within a few metres of the boat, ignoring the bait-shark, which was so freaked out that it seemed intent on jumping back into the boat.

The white shark slowly glided towards the bow of the boat, then turned into a wide circle and rushed at the doomed bait-shark, its powerful tail churning up the water as it gained speed. Within seconds it was closing in, its large jaws opening to display its gleaming rows of teeth. The next moment the shark slammed into its frantically struggling victim with such brutal force that I shuddered at the sheer aggression of the attack, its momentum sending the plastic drum bouncing and skidding across the surface in a spurt of spray and bubbles.

The shark swam off with the bait firmly in its jaws, the drum bobbing along after it. Then the big hook obviously sank deep for the first time. The cable on the trace pulled taut as the shark fled. The drum bounced along behind it for about 20 metres, then disappeared in a plume of spray as the shark went into a dive. By this time, the ratchet on the large reel was screaming its head off as the line rushed out.

I had watched this happen dozens of times, but as always it left me feeling dizzy with excitement to see the awesome power unleashed by a white shark when it attacked the bait-fish and then tried to shake off the hook. Yes, the juices that started flowing when I went into battle with these mighty predators from the deep were definitely the thing that had turned me into a white sharkaholic.

With the adrenaline pumping through my veins I slipped into the fighting chair and strapped myself into the harness, the rod springing to life in my hands even before I had finished hooking it up to the fighting harness. Now the indescribable urge to capture and conquer the creature at the other end of my line took over. That was how it always was, and I have never found a logical explanation for this reaction. One moment I would be mellow and totally relaxed, and the next I would be full of aggression and a stubborn determination to conquer and destroy the enemy I had hooked.

Worried about the rate at which the line was running out, Art frantically tried to hurry me along while at the same time keeping a worried eye on the reel's spool. I told Art to calm down and stop being a pain in the arse; what he should be doing was pulling up the anchor and starting the outboards so that we could follow the shark.

I was ready now, and I locked up the heavy drag, thrilling to the sensation of the harness straps pulling hard at my shoulders in response to the tension on the taut line. Almost immediately the tautening of the line made the hook bite even harder, which brought on a new surge of acceleration by the shark, so powerful that the rod bucked violently and started bending at an acute angle, while the harness straps pulled tight around my shoulders. The relentless pressure squeezed the air out of my lungs and bent my back till it felt as if my spine would snap.

It was time to show the shark who was boss. I braced my legs and leaned into the harness with all my strength in a determined effort to stop it or at least slow it down. It worked – although the massive pressure on my aching back didn't seem to be easing, the speed at which the screaming reel was paying out line slowed down quite significantly.

Having done battle with sharks on so many previous occasions, this let-up didn't fool me into believing that the battle would soon be over. It had only just begun, and I could look forward to one or two hours of fierce combat if I wanted to conquer the great creature that had taken my hook – and believe me, I did want to. I instructed Art to follow the shark slowly and at an angle, then settled into the energy-sapping fight that I knew lay ahead.

By the time Art had lifted anchor and fired up the motors the fleeing shark had stripped off at least 800 metres of line. As usual I was impressed by white sharks' ability to do this sort of thing at high speed while simultaneously dragging along the plastic drum, which obviously caused rather impressive drag on the hook.

I also had the drag on the massive game-fishing reel locked to its maximum, and I was applying as much pressure as was possible, using the full weight of my body. No wonder a person could become so completely addicted to the thrill of doing battle with these very formidable creatures.

The shark and I fought for about 40 minutes before the drum popped out on the surface for the first time, about 100 metres from the boat. Every time this happened during a hunt, the scene of the epic battle with the giant great white shark in the original *Jaws* movie would flash vividly into my mind, and I would experience the most incredible mixture of emotions it is possible to imagine. The controlled fear and exhilaration were like a dizzying drug, so that at such highly special moments I felt as if I was living a dream.

I welcomed the brief respite from the massive pressure on my equipment and shoulders. Art, who was in a highly excited state by now, thought the fight was over and eagerly grabbed the Dacron fishing line to start hauling his trophy closer. This was the wrong move at the wrong time, so I warned him politely: 'You dumb arsehole, what the hell do you think you're doing?'

Just in case he thought I wasn't being polite enough, I explained that the shark was only having a breather and that at any moment now it would rush off again, at which time the line would take his fingers with it. Art hurled the line away as if it had turned into a poisonous snake, and I leaned back into the fighting harness, not only to make sure he never forgot my advice but also to get the shark moving before it had recovered its strength.

The renewed pressure on the hook got an immediate response: the line snapped as taut as a piano wire and the drum disappeared in a shower of spray. But the shark was slowly beginning to weaken under the pressure of drum and rod, and after another 20 minutes of unrelenting struggle it began to show clear signs of exhaustion.

With victory almost achieved, I flexed my aching muscles and started pumping the rod vigorously in a final effort to force the shark into total submission, and five minutes later the struggle was over. The shark rose slowly to the surface and lay wallowing on its side, about eight metres astern.

I estimated the shark at four metres and 800 kilos, so of course there was no question of loading it into the boat, which only weighed 700 kilos itself. Instead we would have to do what shark hunters always did in a case like this, which was to drop a rope with a slipknot around the tail, pull it tight and tow it away. This would reverse-flood the gills and put the shark into a state of paralysis, which would make it easier to tow back and unload in the harbour.

Art wasted no time in responding to my order to haul the shark alongside the boat and drop the rope onto its tail, and while I stood and relaxed amidships he manoeuvred the large grey body to within two metres of the stern of the boat. Then I became aware of an enormous grey triangular object slowly rising to the surface of the calm water some ten metres behind our captive shark.

I stared at it, my mind refusing to register what my eyes were seeing. It was none other than the Submarine, sliding gracefully to the surface almost within spitting distance of us! But then my amazement turned to alarm. The Submarine was not at all interested in our shark: she was heading straight for Art, who was leaning over the stern and hauling our prey closer in order to rope up its tail, totally oblivious of the nightmarish beast closing in on him.

I unglued my tongue to shout a warning, but just then he picked up the movement from the corner of his eye, turned in an abstracted way to see what had caught his attention and ended up looking straight into the gaping jaws of the Submarine, which was now less than two metres from him.

Art reacted in a flash, propelling himself into a sort of backward somersault dive and landing halfway along the deck in spite of the fact that he weighed a good 140 kilos. Then, in what seemed to be the same movement, he set a new backward-crawl world record along the deck till he came up against the console in the bow, where he stopped, frozen with shock. All this, mind you, with a lightning turn of speed that one would not expect from someone of the same general build and appearance as Hagar the Horrible.

As we stood there in stunned silence the Submarine slowly turned her gleaming gunmetal-grey body, passing by the stern with less than a metre to spare and still ignoring the captive shark as it wallowed next to the boat (as she did so I realised once again how massive she really was – she dwarfed the large specimen we had caught to such an extent that it looked like a young shark pup). For a moment it looked as if she was about to swim off and leave us be.

We soon found out that we were very wrong. What actually happened was totally unexpected and I describe it exactly as it occurred. It sounds so unlikely in the retelling that a reader might find it difficult to believe. That is your right, but it would also be your loss, because as far as I know, no one else has ever seen such a thing.

The Submarine might not have been interested in our shark, but our shark, exhausted and severely traumatised though it was, was certainly interested in her and summoned up the energy for a feeble attempt to dive and swim away. The Sub responded by spinning around at great speed and rushing straight at the other shark, dropping her lower jaw.

She slammed squarely into the middle of its back, hitting it with a clearly audible meaty thump and simultaneously locked her massive jaws around the victim's girth; the impact was so powerful that the doomed shark's great body was rammed sideways through the water as it hung out of the Submarine's mouth like a giant crossbow blade, its head to one side and its tail to the other.

All this took only a few seconds, although it seemed as if I was watching the drama unfolding on a movie screen in ultra-slow motion, each moment of it being burned so indelibly into my memory that in later years I never had any trouble in reliving it all, frame by frame, all of them so vivid in my mind that it might have happened only minutes earlier.

Two details I remember particularly well. Firstly, as the Submarine slammed into her victim, the doomed shark actually thrust its jaw forward in a final defiant act. Secondly, the Submarine's mouth was so large that it wrapped almost all the way around the other shark's body, which must have measured at least two and a half metres in circumference, so that only a small portion of the white underbelly protruded from her jaws as she executed her kill.

But more unbelievable sights were to follow. With her victim firmly locked in her jaws, the Submarine dived from the surface in a spectacular plume of spray, dragging her trophy, the terminal trace and the ten-litre drum behind her. Then I became personally involved in the kill.

One moment I was standing in a trance-like state of wonder and shock with my eyes riveted on the Submarine. The next I was ripped off my feet and flung sternwards through the air, crashing painfully into the transom; if I had not been lucky enough to land with my hips jammed between the two outboard motors, there is no doubt that I would have gone overboard.

What had happened, of course, was that I was still holding my rod, which was attached to the harness at one end and to the victim shark at the other via the line and terminal trace, so that when the Submarine went down with our shark in her jaws the line had abruptly tautened and dragged me after her.

My collision with the motors completely winded me and I hung there with the top half of my battered torso overboard, my head only a few inches above the water. Then, as I desperately tried to pull myself up and back, my head and shoulders were dragged violently below the surface before I could fill my lungs with air. Water stung my eyes and rushed into my mouth.

I felt myself pulled deeper by the massive downward pressure on my back and shoulders. I began choking on the water I was involuntarily swallowing and purple spots started flashing before my eyes. Panic gripped me: I was going to drown.

But Art's strong hands gripped me under the arms and hauled my half-drowned body back on board. Totally winded, I lay face down on the deck like a half-drowned rat, gasping for air in between violent coughing and sputtering ... and then, through the foggy haze of discomfort, I heard a muffled but familiar sound: the big reel's ratchet screaming underneath my crumpled body as line raced out of it.

Immediately my hunting instincts kicked in. Although I was still trying to cough the water out of my burning lungs, I heaved myself onto my knees, scrambled into the fighting chair and braced myself against the rod, then leaned in every ounce of the weight I possessed. I was pretty rattled by my near-drowning experience, but the hunter in me was back and he wanted to drag Art's shark away from the Submarine.

The Submarine obliged with 15 minutes of harder fighting than anything I had had with our prey. This was unbelievable stuff, for sure. In my wildest dreams I would never have imagined that any living creature on this planet could grab an 800-kilo shark in its jaws, dive from the surface with it in spite of having to drag a ten-litre drum along as well, and *then* put up a fierce fight in spite of all these impediments.

And it was to become even more unbelievable. I was still distance-wrestling with the Submarine when I decided that it was going to be a really shitty day for me. This was when the line suddenly went limp, so that the rod banged me hard in the face. Only minutes before I had nearly drowned; now I had also acquired a painful bloody nose and had had my pride seriously dented by losing Art's shark to the Submarine.

I turned to Art, shrugging my shoulders in defeat and apology, and I was just about to reassure him that we would come back and fight another day when the water parted in an explosion of spray less than 20 metres from us and the Submarine's huge body burst into sight, going straight up into the air like a Polaris missile with the limp body of our shark still crosswise in her mouth.

We watched, mouths agape, as the Submarine climbed at least three metres into the air. My heart thumped in my chest as I thrilled to this truly unique spectacle. Then she lost her upward momentum. For a moment her gleaming three-ton body hung in the air before slowly rolling over sideways and crashing down into the water again with a boom and a huge splash of spray.

'Suffering shit, am I dreaming?' I shouted at Art, in a voice that I barely recognised, and it dawned on me that he and I were probably the only two people on the planet who had witnessed such a sight, or ever would.

Now I remembered that I was still connected to the Submarine, and braced myself against the harness in anticipation of a renewed struggle. But the line stayed limp. Cursing in disappointment I reeled it in. There was nothing on the end of it – it had parted during the Submarine's spectacular aerobatics.

Up to this moment Art and I had maintained an awed silence, with the exception of that one outburst from me. But now the spell was broken, and we looked at each other as if to confirm that what we had seen and experienced had been real and not a hallucination. Then, still hyped up, we burst into exuberant profanities, and we were still going at it hammer and tongs, when the Submarine gave us a parting present.

Large bubbles and a small slick of some milky white substance, flecked with blood, started drifting to the surface about 20 metres from the boat. Moments later two partially decomposed seal pups popped up in the middle of it. Silent again, we looked on in wide-eyed awe: these were the remnants, courtesy of the Submarine, of the shark we had fought so hard to catch.

Then the plastic drum exploded out of the water. For a moment I thought that the shark's head might still be attached to it, in which case Art would get his jaw after all. But it was not to be. The hook had been torn loose, and all we got back was the steel hook and trace.

When eventually I sat down some 17 years later to write this account, I was amazed that I could still become so charged with a sense of deep-rooted emotion and wonder at what had taken place so long ago. As I recalled those unforgettable memories that were so deeply branded in my mind, I knew that sharing the fullest flavour of this intense real-life drama was beyond my limited writing ability. So I hope that the imagination of my readers will be able to fill the gaps so that justice can be done to my incredible adventure. In the meantime, let me just say: 'Steven Spielberg, eat your heart out!'

FIVE

The shark that just wouldn't die

I had only one more encounter with the Submarine, about two months after the adventure with Art. A German paid me R500, a lot of money at that time, to take him out on a hunt for a great white. We made the usual preparations – chumming, baiting and so on – and sat back to wait. In due course I saw a gargantuan shape gliding through the water and the drum buoy vanished while the line screamed out at such an amazing rate that it was almost all gone by the time I could get to the German's aid and slow it down. But the line snapped and the Submarine got away yet again.

By the end of 1980 my reputation as a white shark hunter had grown to a point where the media were running front-page and feature stories on my escapades off Macassar Beach. Our three hair-raising encounters with the Submarine had just about become folklore – and juicy folklore at that, because the ending hadn't taken place yet.

Headlines like 'Submarine warfare in False Bay', 'Two out to get the Sub' and 'Theo says it's personal with the Sub' helped to publicise my thirst to hook and land the Submarine to the point where – in the popular view, anyway – it was little short of a private war that was so deeply embedded in the public consciousness that to this day people occasionally still ask me what I think happened to my massive opponent.

Thanks to all this journalistic limelight I found myself the target of numerous individuals who wanted to share it, and I was

43

amused when I was accosted by complete strangers who would come up to me and start talking as if they were long-lost cousins or friends. I was more interested, though, in the fact that certain companies had begun showing a lot of interest in my activities and were offering me money and goods in return for displaying their names and logos on my boat and clothing.

This was all well and good, but the new-found fame and status as the fearless (little did they know!) great white shark hunter went straight to my head and soon had me believing that I really was a hero, ridding mankind of the man-eating monsters of the deep. It was balm to my soul, because behind the bravado and bullshit I still suffered from a poor self-image, the result of a fairly abusive childhood (I offer this as an explanation, not an excuse). So yes, it really went to my head.

Up to this time my motivation had been driven by that obsessive passion in me, allied to the need to earn the odd buck or two out of the kill. Now I became a performer of stunts for the media, the public and my sponsors, and instead of seeing myself for what I was, my self-importance became so inflated that I considered it beneath my dignity to hook just any shark that came along.

Nothing less than the really big trophy specimens were worthy of my attention; any great white less than four metres long was too small for me to bother with. I didn't know, and probably would not have cared, that the concerted attack by myself and others – not just in South Africa but elsewhere in the world – on the prime breeding stock was having a negative impact on the future existence of these apex predators, and by extension the ocean's ecological balance.

Now, I was not the first hunter of the great white shark at the Cape. Before my time, in the 1970s *Jaws* era, two brothers called Danie and Stephan Schoeman had become household names in the Gordon's Bay and Strand areas, but they had retired from the field. It was this gap into which I had stepped and revived public interest in the pursuit of the great whites as a result of my various life-threatening experiences.

As I mentioned earlier, the print and broadcasting media were particularly intrigued by my determination to catch the Submarine, and the coverage I received was directly responsible for an approach from the manufacturers of the boat I was using at the time. They offered me its latest design for evaluation on my next Submarine-hunting trip, and of course I accepted right away – given a successful outcome, the chances of a close future relationship would be a sure thing.

Then another development came out of the blue, this time from a journalist who asked me if I was concerned about Stephan Schoeman's challenge regarding the hunting of the Submarine. This was a complete surprise, I replied. I wasn't even aware that the Schoemans had decided to throw their hat into the ring again. But would I be interested in taking them up on it? Well, that was like blood to a shark, so to speak.

'If they want to turn this into a competition or a shark war, let it be so,' I said, playing to the gallery in the style to which I had become accustomed by now. 'I know that this shark and I have an unavoidable date with destiny which has nothing to do with the Schoemans.'

The following Thursday I went along to the boat manufacturers to arrange for picking up the test boat ... only to be told that due to a misunderstanding it had been loaned to Stephan Schoeman. Oh, yeah. He just happened to be going out that weekend with a team of journalists and photographers from *Scope* magazine, then one of the largest-selling popular weeklies in the country.

To say that I was highly pissed off would be a gross understatement. I restrained myself from any excessive display of temper, however, apart from offering the builder some Vaseline to assist him in shoving his boat into a place where the sun didn't shine. Needless to say, this incident only added more fuel to the competition's fire. Any uncertainties about whether it would be fought to the end were now well and truly dispelled. I had a point to make.

Another bag or two of salt was poured into my wounds when Craig, Trevor and I arrived at Gordon's Bay at half past four on the Saturday morning to find the boat manufacturer and Stephan Schoeman preparing to launch their shiny new six-metre craft while the assembled media types looked on in anticipation of a day's adventure.

To my seriously unChristian glee, however, they couldn't get the brand-new outboard motors to start, and while they struggled by torch-light on the slipway we rolled our ten-year-old 5.5-metre boat into the water and fired up its venerable twin Mercury outboards. The faithful Mercuries burst into life at the first turn of the ignition keys and sat there purring like two contented cats. Ha! I could have kissed them.

Ten minutes later we were heading out to sea while the other lot was still trying to breathe life into their dead outboards. It appeared that my offer of a jar of Vaseline would not be needed now after all.

By half past six we had anchored off Macassar Beach and had a steady flow of chum flowing from the back of the boat to advertise the tempting bait-shark we had pulled out of the ocean's larder. Our first customer turned up three hours later, in the shape of a great white about three and a half metres long. I was not after short-arses this morning, however, so I told Trevor to haul the bait out of the water before the shark could actually get at it.

The shark wouldn't leave, however, so when it came up to the boat I grabbed the gaff and gave it a hard jab in the gill area. It took the hint and disappeared in a flurry of swirling water. About 40 minutes later another great white rolled up, a more promising fellow who was at least four metres long and would probably weigh in at about 800 kilos. This was more like it.

The shark didn't waste any time, closing in on the bait and swallowing it on the first cruise-by, then rushing off and diving, buoy and all, when the trace tautened and the hook bit. Full of the day's first adrenaline rush, I climbed onto the fighting chair and was busy strapping my fighting harness to the rod when the drum suddenly popped to the surface. Cursing, I retrieved the trace and found the hook was bare. Clearly it had torn loose, leaving the bait behind as a snack for the great white.

There was nothing to do but re-bait the hook and settle down to wait some more. I wasn't too optimistic about a third encounter, given our crappy luck so far. Still, I told myself, you never knew: just this once we might have lightning striking in the same place again. All that positive thinking didn't do me much, good, though. It was clearly shaping up to be one of those bad-luck days.

Then, as I sat there feeling sorry for myself, the buoy was ripped from the surface of the water with no warning at all, and moments later the large reel on the rod started screaming. We were back in business! I hurled myself into the fighting chair, and the fight was on as I tried to control the fleeing shark. But after about 15 minutes of frenzied action the line snapped and off went the shark with my special hook, eight metres of steel cable and the 25-litre drum buoy.

Shit, shit, shit! I was now so peeved and frustrated that I came close to throwing the rod overboard in utter frustration. Three sharks in less than two hours, and nothing to show for it! I just wasn't used to such dismal failure, and I was cheesed off to the point where I was on the verge of packing up and going home. The only thing that persuaded me to stay and try again was the fact that Schoeman's boat was anchored no more than 500 metres away and so far had not even seen a great white, never mind hooked one.

He and his entourage were quite a sight. He had had to give up on the test craft because its outboards simply couldn't be got to work, so there he lay in his little 4.7-metre workaday boat with the *Scope* team packed into it like sardines. That was enough for me. I told Craig to start chumming again and got to work assembling a new terminal rig. I had everything to gain and nothing to lose.

And before long I gained it. Another four-metre great white came cruising in and swallowed the bait in one smooth motion, with the usual consequences, and we spent about an hour in one hell of a fight before it hoisted the white flag and we dropped a rope around its tail. All this time Schoeman was sitting high and dry without a bite, so it was not surprising that at that moment I felt like an alpha male dog with a whole avenue full of trees to lift his leg against.

The course I was steering would take us past Schoeman's boat, and – spiteful son of a bitch that I was – I decided to rub some salt into *their* wounds by passing as close as possible. Okay, it wasn't the Submarine I was towing, but it was a good-sized shark all the same, and a lot better than nothing.

My elated crew and I were drawing abreast of Schoeman's boat when he hailed us to come closer. Apologetically he said that because he hadn't scared up a single great white, the photographers would like to take shots of the one we had in tow. I agreed and manoeuvred our shark in as close to Schoeman's boat as we possibly could, then preened myself while the shutters clicked away.

But pride goeth before a fall, and the photographers got more than they bargained for. Clearly thinking that the shark wallowing alongside his boat was dead – which it certainly seemed to be – Schoeman leaned over the side with his gaff and hooked it in the head. It immediately became clear that the shark was anything but dead, and some big-time drama instantly followed.

In a flash the formerly dead-looking shark arched its back and reared out of the water between Schoeman's motors, aiming straight at him, so that for a moment it was touch and go as to whether he would end up in its jaws or not. That aside, the consequences of its landing in the jam-packed boat itself were too awful to contemplate, and I slammed my motors into gear and towed the shark out of range.

The journalists were, to judge by their expressions, in a state of well-nigh terminal shock and bemusement, and I couldn't blame them. Having a four-metre great white shark land in your lap is a hell of a way to enjoy a fishing trip.

When we arrived back at Gordon's Bay and started to unload the great white shark the boat manufacturer came over from his dysfunctional tub and gave me a thousand words, strongly redolent of bullshit, about why he had handed the boat to Schoeman. I wasn't in a forgiving mood yet, and I told him: 'When you give your word, you keep it. You didn't, so just piss off and leave me alone.'

I didn't know it then, but my career as a hunter of great whites was soon to undergo a drastic change ... and, like many other moments in my life, it did so without warning. But it would have such a profound effect on me that I would never be the same again, and it would influence the course of my life as dramatically as that first face-to-face encounter with the shark on the rocks of the Natal south coast.

It all started on a perfect day in the early autumn of April 1981 while we were out on one of our trips after a great white (and, who knows, maybe even my old opponent the Submarine). This particular hunt started in typical fashion when I steered the boat over to my happy hunting grounds off Macassar Beach and told Anton, a new crew member, to drop anchor and start chumming while I fished for suitable bait.

It was one of those mild sunny days you get in late autumn when the Cape's fickle weather is behaving itself; there was not a breath of wind and the flat, shiny sea looked like a gigantic oil slick. In a word, perfect conditions for hunting sharks. I was filled with contentment as I sat back, glancing occasionally at the plastic drum buoy bobbing gently whenever the bait-fish, a small shark, tugged at it. Life just didn't get much better than this. Not only was the weather beautiful, but I was confident that a white shark would soon put in an appearance.

I seemed to have developed a sort of sixth sense about these matters, so that on many occasions I would feel a fluttering in my stomach and an almost uncontrollable excitement building inside of me just before a great white made an appearance. It happened so often that eventually it became common for Craig and the crew members who knew about it to ask if I had the 'vibe', and when I said I did, I was almost invariably right.

On this day I started to get the 'vibe' about 20 minutes after we had set up. I told my crew, and sure enough, within a few minutes the buoy started jumping around as the bait-fish attached to it announced the arrival of a shark. The lazy relaxed mood on board changed instantly into one of urgency and excited anticipation as Anton and I concentrated our attention on the drum, which was now doing a frenzied jig behind the boat.

Moments later, a great white came cruising into view. It was a big one, over four metres long and in outstanding condition, and my pulse quickened as I ran my eyes down that beautifully proportioned body. The new arrival wasted no time in making its intentions clear. A slash of the powerful tail sent it homing in on the doomed bait-shark, which it devoured in a gulp. Then, as expected, the great white ran for it when the hook began to bite. It was a real fighter (just how much of a fighter I didn't realise) and it was two hours before it gave up. We dropped a rope over its tail, tied the end to a cleat and set off in high spirits on the leisurely 40-minute cruise back to Gordon's Bay.

We got there without mishap, entered the small harbour and slowly negotiated our way around the small craft lying at their floating moorings till we reached the small-craft jetty. I cut the motors, allowing the boat to come to a gentle stop against the fenders, and got ready to climb out and onto the jetty.

Just then the boat started swaying from side to side. What the hell was going on? I looked around and was stunned to see the supposedly dead or dying shark thrashing and straining against the rope that secured its tail to the boat. I couldn't understand it. We had towed the shark backwards for at least ten kilometres, and at the least it should have been virtually lifeless from the reverse flushing of its gills.

For some reason, however, this one was a lethal exception to the rule, and now we were in serious trouble. Without immediate evasive action this 800-kilo-plus mass of muscle with its murderous teeth would almost certainly land up in the boat with us.

I dived over to the controls, shouted to Anton to drop the bowline and fired up the motors. I thumped them into gear and swung the boat away from the jetty so that we could tow the highly agitated shark out to the open sea. As I cleared the breakwater I relayed our unexpected crisis to the harbourmaster on the radio, and almost immediately my friend Art came on the air, obviously having monitored my call at his base station back at his home.

He had a harpoon specially designed to deal with hard-arsed great whites like this one, he said, and he would be at the harbour with it in ten minutes so that we could settle my problem customer's hash. This suited me fine, so I towed the shark around in wide circles till Art's dilapidated old van arrived and his familiar bearded bulk erupted from it, sudden-death harpoon in hand, and took up station on a moored fishing boat. I blipped the throttles and came back in, heading directly for the boat on which Art was waiting. Obeying his shouted instructions, I brought the shark as close as I could to him, and he plunged the harpoon into the side of its head with such energy that the point went right through and came out of the side.

Instead of giving up the ghost, the shark reacted with such a violent jerk that Art almost ended up in the water. Blood

51

pumped freely out of the gaping wound in its head and turned the water around us a gory red, but, incredibly, the shark showed no signs of dying or even weakening. I took the boat into another turn to give Art a second opportunity with his harpoon. This didn't work either, and neither did a third attempt, and when Art speared the white shark for the fourth time the harpoon's staff snapped.

We had attracted a number of spectators by now, and one of them offered me his .38 Special revolver. I didn't want to fire any shots inside the harbour, so we towed the bleeding shark back out to about 50 metres beyond the end of the breakwater. When I was completely satisfied that there was no danger to any people or property I took careful aim and fired five rounds into the shark's head.

To my considerable relief it stopped struggling and wallowed lifelessly behind the boat. What a fighter! It had turned what should have been a normal and well-executed kill into something resembling an all-out war. In a calmer frame of mind, I towed the shark back into the harbour, where we loaded the great limp body onto the boat trailer and towed it out of the water to the top of the slipway.

An amazing amount of blood was still oozing out of the shark from its many wounds as it lay on the slipway inside a large and distinctly festive-spirited ring of spectators. I moved in close to check up on the damage done by the .38 Special bullets, noticing that one had apparently damaged the muscles behind the shark's right eye, which was now hanging lopsided in its socket.

I was still intently inspecting the damage when Art decided, for some reason best known to himself, to poke his finger into the damaged eye while getting ready to produce one of the wise-guy witticisms he liked to utter. We were robbed of the benefit of his wit, however, when the battered, shot-up, bleeding shark corpse came back to life *again*, thrashing violently from side to side and gnashing its fearsome teeth; leaping back, I caught sight of its good eye and was stunned to see that it still had the shiny glint of a creature that was not yet ready to die.

I was seized with sudden rage and a growing embarrassment at the shark's refusal to give in to death. 'What in God's name must I do to kill this damn shark?' I shouted, snatching the sharp bait-knife from my waistband and stabbing it deep into the flesh at the base of its spine. I hacked at its tormented flesh till (and it was a relief) the blade finally severed the spinal cord. Now the great body went limp for the last time, its defiant spark of life snuffed out forever, and when I looked at its undamaged eye again the glint of life had been replaced by the milky haze of death.

And now, as I stood over the shark's body, executioner's knife in hand and smeared with its blood, I became aware of something strange and almost frightening: for the first time since I had landed the ragged-tooth all those years ago, there was no exultation or feeling of self-importance in my heart. Instead I felt confused and ashamed that I had had to slaughter a defiant shark in order to conquer it.

It was a shattering moment during which my entire reason for being began to crumble away. I had grown up with and endorsed the belief that sharks were brainless eating machines that patrolled the ocean in search of victims. They had no right to existence; the only good shark was a dead one. And now my uncomplicated little world was being turned upside down by this stupid shark's refusal to play the game by my rules. It had put up such a fierce fight to survive that I actually felt disturbed and slightly humbled.

I went home in a thoughtful mood, although I hadn't yet realised that the desperate battle and then finally the messy execution of this enormous sea creature had brought me to a spiritual crossroads. Theo Ferreira, arrogant and cocky slayer of sharks, had turned a corner and set foot on a new journey from which there would be no turning back.

A number of individuals, myself included, could claim some credit for the legislation that, approximately eight years after this life-changing moment, gave official protection to the great white sharks in the waters off the South African coastline. But the first and most vital role-player in this success was that nameless predator, the one that had refused to die, and in doing so unwittingly began a process that would play a vital role in the future of great white sharks, both in South African waters and elsewhere in the world. A new era had dawned.

It took me quite a long time to work out what was happening to me. I went on putting to sea as before, always with my special shark-hunting equipment at the ready, but although I often encountered large great whites I never again put a baited terminal trace into the water. And I stayed my hand without a moment's regret, because the desire to hunt and kill the great whites had disappeared altogether.

I found it hard to explain the exact reason, not only to others but to myself. It was a strange and extremely frustrating situation. I was still as much of a sharkaholic as I had ever been; at the same time, I didn't have the least desire to hunt them. Much thinking brought me to one of the better conclusions of my life: I would not try to kick the addiction, but I would put my shark-hunting equipment away for good, and instead start observing and interacting with these marvellous creatures of the blue water.

It was my introduction to a fascinating world to which I had been blind during my sharking-killing years. In spite of all my forays I had actually had very little visual contact with them. Once a shark made its appearance it would normally waste little time before homing in on the baited hook. After that, hunter and hunted fought their deadly duel at a distance; the only time you really saw the shark was when it was dragged from the water, by which time it was either dead or dying – a mere shadow of its vital self.

Now I found myself plunged into the great whites' world, interacting with and observing them at close quarters and for extended periods. It was incredibly exciting and rewarding. My old dogmatic attitude toward the great whites underwent a complete about-face, stirring into life new emotions and feelings I had not even realised I possessed. My long-held misconceptions were replaced by a new respect and understanding of their complex behaviour. From there it was a natural step to hit the books for a bit of do-it-yourself education, and then I discovered the vital role that sharks played in the ocean's ecosystem.

My new-found knowledge and attitude were to be tested towards the latter part of the 1980s, when several shark attacks along the South African coastline triggered great publicity and fear among Cape people, who have always tended to believe, all evidence to the contrary, that shark attacks were things that happened mainly along the KwaZulu-Natal coast or further afield.

An attack that caused particular agitation took place near the small seaport town of Mossel Bay on the south coast, when a swimmer named Nico von Broembsen was savaged while surfing in the area known as the Point. A badly bitten Von Broembsen was rushed to hospital in a serious condition after being washed ashore, and Mossel Bay mayor Johan Oosthuizen put a bounty on the shark's head in the true *Jaws* tradition.

The moment I read about this in the newspapers I contacted Mr Oosthuizen and warned him that a free-for-all bounty-hunt on the local shark population would do more harm than good.

The shark in question, I explained, would be one of the fairly large number of great whites that patrolled this bay and nearby Seal Island, which had a large fur seal population. A bunch of amateur white shark hunters, armed with inadequate equipment and pouring uncontrolled quantities of blood and chum mixtures into the water, would be a recipe for disaster: it would almost certainly result in a number of large predator sharks swimming around in his bay, injured and pretty pissed off.

Allowing hundreds of litres of blood and chum to be washed around by the currents in the bay, I went on, would be the equivalent of creating a supermarket for the great whites, with numbers of highly stimulated predators hunting down the food source that their finely tuned senses would be homing in on. That was bad news for humans swimming anywhere close by.

Mr Oosthuizen got the message: by putting up a bounty he had created a potential powder keg that could very easily blow up in his hands. How should he go about cancelling the shark hunt without too much loss of face for the town council? I thought about it and suggested a public announcement to inform all concerned of the danger to public safety if there was uncontrolled and indiscriminate shark hunting in the bay.

His response was: 'Why don't you come down here and hunt this murdering shark yourself?' My first reaction was to turn him down flat; those days were long behind me. But when I considered the results of uncontrolled hunting, I realised that the sacrifice of one creature could save many lives.

So I accepted, but made it clear that I did not expect payment for anything except my travel and living expenses, because I would *not* become involved in anything that smacked of *Jaws*-style bounty hunting. Mr Oosthuizen agreed, and I packed my bags and headed for Mossel Bay.

I spent seven days in Mossel Bay on a boat supplied by the municipality and crewed by two of its workers, who probably thought at first that I was mad. Our chumming in the attack area attracted several young great whites, not one longer than three and a half metres, and to the confusion and vocal protests of my crewmen I positively refused to catch them – the bait would be whipped out of the water and we would prod and bully the shark till it went on its way. Each time I'd explain to my faithless followers that the shark we were looking for would be almost two metres longer and about 300 kilos heavier than these tiddlers. Whether they believed me was another matter.

But on the third morning a five-metre white shark glided into view 20 metres from the boat. I realised immediately that its jaw pattern would almost certainly match the tooth-marks left on Von Broembsen's torn body, and I jumped into action.

I knew that the shark had been attracted by the chum slick and would probably stay in the area as long as it kept flowing, so I told my underlings to stay at it while I carefully secured a large bait-fish to the hook before dropping it overboard with the terminal trace and 25-litre drum buoy. Then I made ready to do battle, just as I had done so many times before in my former life as a hunter-killer.

As I did so I became aware of a ski boat rushing directly down on us, and recognised it as one that had been lying about 500 metres from us all morning. *These curious local yokels are going to get in the way and bugger up this kill,* I thought angrily, catching the skipper's eye – they were less than 50 feet from us at this stage – and waving him off.

The idiot ignored my waving as well as my verbal protests, which were not as polite as a well-bred person might have wished, and their next actions showed that I had been mistaken, and that it was not just simple-minded curiosity that had brought them trespassing on my patch of ocean.

They bore down on the drum buoy till they were almost on top of it and then, to my renewed fury, tossed a big stockfish attached to a large hook and chain overboard. I got even madder when they followed this with a 200-litre steel drum. The damn fools were trying to steal our shark from under our noses.

I wound myself up to warn them off with threats of serious bodily harm when the shark put an abrupt end to the argument. The steel drum suddenly started bouncing and skimming along the surface in the direction of the reef that forms part of the Point area. The four coffee-bar cowboys raced off in hot pursuit with whoops of triumph and boastful jeers about grabbing the killer right in front of the big shark hunter.

I was really pissed off by all this, but I told my makeshift crew to get the anchor up at the double so that we could catch up with these arseholes before all hell broke loose: if they tried to land or manhandle the fleeing shark they would be likely to find themselves on the receiving end, no place to be when the injured party was a fed-up great white capable of biting their little ski boat in half.

By the time we got underway the four clowns and my hijacked shark were already about 700 metres away, but I gunned the motors and managed to reduce the gap to about 200 metres. Then I realised it was just about mango-in-fan time and abruptly throttled back, so that our boat glided to a stop. This baffled my ignorant crew all over again, but the shark saved me the trouble of explaining.

We (and especially my crewmen) watched in fascination as the steel drum was dragged directly into the path of the large swells, which were racing on to the nearby reef to form a set of perfect six-foot crashing waves. It was as if my white shark was choosing the exact route of the attack on Von Broembsen.

Oblivious to what was about to happen, the four comedians rushed on behind the shark in a gay abandon born of total ignorance. Moments later, however, they started learning the hard way about the seriousness of life when the drum headed straight into the first large swell.

The swell was in the process of transforming itself into an almost vertical two-metre wave, a veritable wall of water. The drum hit it, came to a dead stop and reversed course, and then the shark's huge head and equally huge upper body shot straight up out of the water. The weight of the drum ripped the hook out of the shark's mouth and it made for the open sea at a rate of knots.

And that was that. I didn't see another shark of any kind for the next four days, so I told Mr Oosthuizen I was packing it in because there wasn't a sign of a great white in the bay.

That was the last shark attack at Mossel Bay for 18 months. Then a young woman named Monique Price became the next victim. Unlike Von Broembsen, she paid with her life. As I heard the story, a retired farmer named Hennie Terblanche had lost his boat's anchor a couple of days earlier and went off to see if he could retrieve it, taking Monique Price, her fiancé and a friend along for the ride. The young people were diving for the anchor when she was hit by a large great white, which mauled her in the leg and pelvic area. Terblanche rushed her to the local hospital, but she died of shock and massive loss of blood.

Presumably Mr Oosthuizen still remembered my advice, because this time there was no sign of the *Jaws* mentality; no bounties were offered and my telephone remained silent.

SIX

The turning point

Towards the end of 1989 I was relaxing at home when my eyes fell on a local newspaper article that reported that the well-known Dolphin Action Protection Group, which was headed by dedicated conservationist Mrs Nan Rice, had conducted an opinion poll on the public attitude towards having the great white shark declared a protected species. To say that my socks were knocked off by the result would be putting it mildly. Almost 85 per cent of the 180 people interviewed were in favour of protection.

That really made me sit up and take notice. According to the article there was a worldwide concern that the species was in danger of becoming extinct owing to exploitation. It also quoted Dr Leonard Compagno of the South African Museum on how slowly the species matured, and what a vital role it played in maintaining the natural balance in the oceans.

The information turned my world upside down. I had already stopped hunting great whites in favour of observing them, but the switch had stemmed from a strictly subjective personal motivation. Now I had been hit with objective facts and figures, and introduced for the first time to the knowledge that there was a sudden worldwide concern about the white shark's future existence if the wanton destruction did not stop.

A lot of things started falling into place, and, without my knowing it, I was on the threshold of yet another stage of my personal development. I had started as a rip-roaring killer of great whites. From there I had gone on to become a passive observer of their mysterious world. Now I was about to turn from passive observer to passionate conservationist.

It dawned on me for the first time in my life that, without doubt, my blissful hunts of the fairly recent past had contributed to the great white sharks' perilous situation, and suddenly I was weighed down by guilt. The only way to deal with guilt is by atoning, and in my book that meant doing something concrete, not just indulging in public breast-beating.

How to go about turning my Damascus experience into something worthwhile was another matter. I couldn't see myself becoming a bunny-hugging conservationist wimp. Damn it all, I was still the same old hairy-chested Theo Ferreira with a reputation to uphold and protect! I indulged in some serious soul-searching that swept aside the excuses I had been hiding behind and forced myself to take personal stock. I knew I would have to make a conscious stand for what I believed in. After this it was much easier to find the courage to do something positive about the plight of the great whites.

I also knew what I had to do next. In August 1989 I began collaborating with Nan Rice and Len Compagno in the campaign to raise public awareness about the need to protect the species, and soon afterwards found myself taking a leading role in lobbying the Department of Environmental Affairs and Sea Fisheries. I was not starry-eyed about any of these activities, and did not hesitate to tell my collaborators that it was a crazy venture in which we did not have a hope in hell of achieving any success. But I went at it hammer and tongs all the same.

No doubt this sounds somewhat illogical, but I had it clearly worked out. Saving the global great white shark population was something that simply had to be done, no matter how difficult it might be, and someone had to try to do it ... someone who had plenty of pig-headed determination to sustain him when – as appeared likely – there was a long and potholed road ahead.

That person was Theo Ferreira, well-known glutton for punishment, defender of the underdog (or underfish, I suppose you could say in this case) and ever-willing volunteer to play David in the inevitable struggle with the official Goliath. And struggle it was; I soon discovered that the great white shark affair had all the elements of a major battle.

My new-found courage and belief in myself made me outspoken with the authorities and other role-players in the great white shark arena, and I was amazed to find that the people I was dealing with were actually sitting up and taking notice of what I was saying.

For instance, Len Compagno told me that little was known about the natural behaviour of great white sharks along the South African coastline because there was no existing body of field research.

My immediate response was to suggest that such a research project be launched, and he pledged his encouragement and backing if I could get something like this up and running, indicating that he would be very interested in acting as the project's scientific advisor.

His enthusiasm was catching, and I was very excited at the thought of such a challenging mandate. I decided there and then to grab it with both hands, although I knew nothing about white shark research or how to launch a project of this nature. So I jumped in at the deep end and swam for all I was worth, and almost immediately there was a result.

Within days I was called to a meeting with the directors of the South African Museum, where Len Compagno and I proposed launching what we called the 'White Shark Research Project' (WSRP). Together, we must have put up a convincing argument: it was agreed that the project could be housed temporarily at the museum, although Dr Michael Cluver, one of the museum directors, made it clear that this arrangement was only possible because of Len's involvement.

It was also made clear to me that the South African Museum would not involve itself financially in the project, which I found a bit strange. Here we had a research project with the prestige of the South African Museum and a world-renowned scientist behind it, but it didn't have a cent in the bank nor one piece of logistical equipment to its name. But I didn't brood on it. Unless the WSRP got hold of some cash in a hurry there was a very real danger that it would die before it was even fully conceived. I would have to make a plan, and fast.

As I had done so often in the past, I started by turning to the one person who would, I knew, willingly and unconditionally back me to the hilt in any venture: Norma – wife, best friend and very special person. True to form, Norma gave me R3 000 for seed money from the meagre earnings of a pine bed manufacturing business which she ran from our home. I used it to print 2 000 bumper stickers and 100 sweatshirts bearing the logo 'Save the white shark'.

I am filled with sadness when I reflect now on how I was so wrapped up in the project that I never took the time to look into her eyes and tell her how humbly grateful I was for her support over this entire formative period of the WSRP, and in fact during the many years we shared together. She was the glue that held me together, the substance in my life. I often ask myself: *Where would you have been without Norma?*

Over the following six weeks, my three teenage children sold the merchandise to the public, turning the initial investment of R3 000 into R26 000, which went straight into a bank account opened by the museum, to be used by them for administration and control on behalf of the WSRP. At the same time, Len prepared a funding proposal for the South African Nature Foundation. Dr Allan Heydorn of the SANF was very enthusiastic. He indicated that he believed the WSRP project was worthwhile, and that approving the funding for the project would be a mere formality.

This meeting with the SANF was so positive that Len and I were quite certain the funding would be forthcoming, so we started calling for quotes for the boat and research equipment that would be needed. But about six weeks later the SANF informed us that it was rejecting the proposal. It was a devastating shock, coming after the positive reception given to the proposal, and it knocked the legs out from under the WSRP because we had all but stopped our fundraising activities.

And the story got worse. Following the SANF's thumbs-down, Len and the museum directors indicated that they wanted to drop their involvement in the project. I was bitterly disappointed with the SANF for its sudden about-face, but it was not in my nature simply to roll over and play dead. I paid an unannounced visit to the SANF head office and tackled Dr Heydorn and one of his colleagues. After a long conversation, I finally realised that for some reason they had had a change of heart. It was also clear that I could expect no further support from that quarter.

My disappointment was so great that I actually began asking myself whether I had not bitten off more than I could chew this time. This really wasn't like me at all, and it took an event I wasn't even involved in to yank my normal resolve back from wherever it had gone, namely, the WSRP's first white shark research trip of sorts.

As it happened I couldn't go along – possibly a good thing, considering my mood. But Craig, Len and Mike Boon, another WSRP team member, were available and they had a real adventure that was to have an unexpected effect.

The catalyst for this first venture was one PJ van der Walt, who turned up out of the blue one Wednesday when Craig and Mike were at the Shark Centre of the South African Museum, busy sorting out slides for a school lecture.

As Craig tells it, 'I received a phone call from Security to tell me that there was a guy who called himself PJ waiting at the front desk. He wanted to come up and talk about sharks ... PJ turned out to be an interesting guy who had been doing the odd white shark cage dive trip at Dyer Island and in False Bay for the past couple of years.

'He said that Dyer Island was great for sharks, but that it was too far from Cape Town, so he had spent the past three months looking for sharks in False Bay, but without any luck. PJ asked if we had any advice about False Bay. I asked him where he had been trying and it seemed like he was working in the correct areas.

'This confused me, as my father and I had almost always found white sharks in these areas when we went out to hunt them. In fact, as far as I was concerned, Macassar Beach in False Bay was one of the best places in the world to find great white sharks. So PJ asked if we wanted to join him on a trip that Saturday as he had some clients and perhaps we could assist him in finding sharks.'

Craig was amenable to the idea, and he, Len and Mike agreed to meet PJ at Gordon's Bay early on the Saturday morning for what turned out to be a very good trip, although the day didn't get off to a good start because there was no sign of PJ, either then or considerably later. Here is Craig's account of what happened:

PJ had told us to be at the harbour by six am sharp and it was now approaching half past eight, so Len, Mike and I were not happy, especially since nobody could get hold of the elusive Mr PJ van der Walt ... We were on our third cup of coffee and I do not think the caffeine was helping our deteriorating mood.

Our motivation for sticking around for him was the fact that the White Shark Research Project had just been formed and we did not even have a research boat to do work from. Any opportunity we could find to get on the water had to be grabbed, and in fact, this was the first trip we were doing as a research team.

Other than PJ's no-show it was nice to be in Gordon's Bay. The harbour is small, with a naval officers' training centre, a marina, coffee shops and curio shops, and I loved it because it brought back all the memories of the days when we had hunted the giant great whites of False Bay.

Then the captain of the old wooden trawler PJ had chartered came over and said that PJ had phoned and was on his way. We went off to have breakfast at the harbour shop and PJ arrived about an hour later. He came over and said, 'Sorry I'm a bit late, but I had heaps to organise.' When I'm aggravated I tend to become confrontational, so I told him that if he wanted to waste time he should leave us out of it. This was not a good start to our day.

Anyway, we chugged out of the harbour just after ten 'o clock, and I told the captain to head for Macassar Beach. The wind was a light onshore, so I directed him to find 22 metres and anchor about two miles from the beach. We had about nine miles to cover and the boat was slow, so I went up on to the cabin roof to get a better view of the flat surface of the ocean. Just being out on the water helped to put us all back in a good mood and those massive mountains, which stood like guards over the bay, were just breathtaking. After a few deep breaths of the ocean air, all felt great.

Just over an hour later we were close to where I wanted the boat to anchor and right there, about 300 metres from the boat and a little to the left, I saw the shadow of a 2.5-metre-long white shark cruising on the surface. I stomped my foot on the cabin roof to get PJ's attention. Almost instantly his head popped out of the window and I told him about the shark, which was still cruising towards the beach.

PJ became so excited that it was difficult to tell him what to do and where to anchor the boat. After much screaming, shouting and pointing we managed to get the boat anchored upstream from where the shark was last seen. It had gone deeper by now. On the stern a tornado erupted as PJ went into crazy mode with his baits and chum. PJ had the best chum I had ever seen, five 25-litre cans of whale oil, a bin of seal-chunks and another with chunks of whale blubber.

I decided to stay on the roof while PJ and his assistant went to work with the chum. While I was impressed by the quality of it, I was not keen on getting up close and personal, especially since PJ was literally covering the entire deck with it. I could not believe my eyes as PJ and his assistant stumbled and slid around that oil-covered deck. There is absolutely nothing like whale oil for slipperiness, and once it is underfoot you are on oiled ice. Although it was a comedy show, I liked it – PJ with his strong character and incredible excitement made it quite enjoyable.

PJ decanted about ten litres of the oil into a bucket, which he then emptied into the ocean. The oil spread out into a spectacular slick; it looked as though an oil tanker had just sunk off our stern. It immediately started to drift away from the boat, towards the shore, and after five minutes it was already quite far from the boat, so I asked PJ when he was going to put more chum in. He said that he did it every ten minutes or so.

This was why he was not getting the sharks. The big chum pool was drifting away from the boat and taking the sharks with it. Without finding a source to the chum, the sharks were just following it and swimming around within it till they became bored and moved on.

I told PJ this and suggested that he take one can, make a small hole in it and dangle it over the side where it would slowly drip into the water. I also said that he would only need about ten to 20 litres of the oil for the entire day. I could see that he did not want to be told what to do, but his luck had not been good over the past months, and so he reluctantly obliged.

Within an hour we had five great white sharks at the boat. Two were around 2.5 metres long, one was about 2.8 metres and another was close to three metres. The fifth was a large female we named 'Notch Fin', due to the peculiar pattern on the trailing edge of her dorsal fin. Notch Fin touched around 3.8 metres, although she was obviously still young.

While PJ was going nuts in the stern with his whale oil and chunks of seal, we stayed out of his way and concentrated on recording dominant and hierarchical behaviour on the part of the sharks. The water visibility was only a metre or two, so that it was not possible to see the sharks or what they were doing unless they were near the surface, but we still managed to make some very interesting observations.

Before Notch Fin arrived, we had two smaller sharks at the boat, readily approaching the baits on the end of the ropes, swimming beneath the hull and coming up to the dive platform. PJ was extremely excited as he began getting his punters ready to dive in the cage off the stern while both sharks calmly swam around just below the surface ten metres off our transom. Then somebody flicked the switch and they were gone.

Replacing them was Notch Fin, and she came in like a steam train, without any hesitation. We could clearly see the difference in her behaviour, compared to the other sharks. She was bold, agitated, and immediately laid into the baits on the lines, taking two chunks of seal before anyone had a chance to grab the ropes and pull them away from her.

Notch Fin had obviously decided that the boat belonged to her, and immediately made it clear that she had absolutely no intention of sharing her bounty with any of the others. Some smaller sharks arrived after her and initially kept a respectful distance, but then one of them, a male of about 2.5 metres in length, became very bold and repeatedly made attempts to approach the boat and baits.

Notch Fin would hang around the boat for a few minutes and then swim off, and as soon as she did this the smaller shark would approach. Within a minute Notch Fin would be back to chase him away, and he would cruise along the surface at a respectful distance of about 50 metres off the stern till Notch Fin wandered off again. Then he would try again. The other three sharks stayed clear of the boat, even when Notch Fin went away, but the chancer would pounce as soon as Notch Fin's back was turned.

What still intrigues me today is how they knew where they and the other sharks were in spite of the poor visibility. The small shark would be 50 metres away, but when Notch Fin went off he would cruise in. How did he know that she had left?

This went on for a while, and then Notch Fin came in once again and took yet another chunk of seal, dived under the boat and came up on the port side before finally swimming around the bow and back down towards the stern of the boat, where she dived out of sight. At this point, the small male was cruising on the surface, about 40 metres off the stern, slightly to the left.

Then the water suddenly exploded under him as Notch Fin attacked from below, ripping so savagely into his gut that he was lifted right into the air, and then shook her head violently from side to side. The water around him instantly went red as the male's midsection opened up, so that his blood and entrails emptied into the ocean in a great pool of froth and disturbance. On the boat, we watched all this happen in stunned silence.

The attack ended as abruptly as it had begun. Notch Fin disappeared as soon as she had struck the deathblow, leaving the dying juvenile to thrash briefly and then sink out of sight. Seconds later she was back at the boat, going for the baits and behaving as if nothing had happened.

We deduced from this awe-inspiring incident that great whites definitely had some form of social hierarchy, and over the next few years that first impression was confirmed by a number of similar observations. On the surface we could see only the very tip of the iceberg, of course, while below this mantle there were obviously all sorts of exciting interactions taking place.

Notch Fin had quite obviously claimed our boat as her territory and was able to maintain dominance because she was the largest shark. We are quite confident that the attack on the ill-fated juvenile male was not a simple random act of aggression. He did not pay Notch Fin sufficient respect on that day, but she did not attack till she had given him more than enough warnings to back off.

Len, Mike and I returned home elated and full of inspiration to find more funding for our small and very poor research team so that we could carry out the work we felt was so important.

I was ecstatic when I heard about the fantastic day the embryonic WSRP team had had, and their excitement immediately rubbed off on me. My self-doubt vanished like mist in the morning and I became even more determined than I had been to make the WSRP work. We had come so far on our own and we wouldn't let go of this wonderful challenge.

For starters, I made contact with the Mazda Wildlife Fund, which was actively promoting its image by supporting wildlife research and conservation projects. I telephoned Gerhard Visser, the fund coordinator, and told him that Mazda had a unique opportunity to become involved with the most feared, mysterious and least-researched apex predator species on the planet.

Somehow, I must have touched some of the right buttons with my impassioned plea, because within a week the fund had sent him to Cape Town to evaluate us. Visser indicated that

Mazda was keen on the project, but added that our application would take about three months to process.

I was very grateful for the interest, but the thought of waiting three whole months with the possibility of being turned down again at the end of it was a heavy burden. I decided to start working on a Plan B while I waited for Mazda to make up its mind. If Mazda decided against funding me, that would be that and I would still have another string to my bow. If Mazda said yes, it would be a bonus.

So two weeks after applying to Mazda I submitted a proposal to the provincial and national education authorities to gain approval for launching a national schools white shark fundraising drive and education programme that would have something for everybody, since there would be cash prizes for the top schools, ranging from R15 000 down to R1 000.

Much red tape and careful screening later they came to the party, and 150 schools from around the country were invited to participate in the fundraising drive. In the end the challenge was taken up by 137 schools, which meant that more than 280 000 pupils throughout South Africa were involved.

It was a monumental task for an organisation as small and poorly funded as the WSRP, but my entire team, especially Craig, Tracy and Mike Boon, expended much blood, sweat and tears to get the scheme off the ground. The kids went at it with a will, and after all the prize money and expenses had been paid, more than R45 000 went into the WSRP's bank account.

I felt real gratitude towards those youngsters, who had set an example to the SANF, Mazda and the rest of South Africa by showing that they cared and were willing to do something to protect this vital part of our national heritage. So, belatedly, I would like to say a sincere 'thank you' to each of those young people (or rather their adult selves of today), as well as the schools and, of course, the members of the public who played such a vital role in getting the project up and running.

The competition was such a resounding success that we negotiated with the authorities to continue the WSRP's involvement
with schools on a national basis, with the WSRP involved in
creating educational programmes for school use nationwide.
This proposal was enthusiastically accepted and a National
Schools Education Programme was launched by the WSRP in
January 1992.

The WSRP would visit the involved schools on a voluntary
basis and present lectures and slide-shows on the role of the
white shark in the ocean's ecosystem. Each participating school
would also select a group of five pupils and a teacher to join
the WSRP on a five-day field data collecting trip. This project
proved to be a great success, and many schools sent groups to
join our team at sea. This very rewarding and stimulating work
afforded all involved the opportunity to work and interact with
the magnificent predators.

The people at Mazda were so impressed with the results of
the schools campaign and the interest shown by the educational
authorities they decided to improve their initial offer of support,
which was for the loan of a Mazda utility vehicle to the WSRP.
Now they also agreed to pay off the R48 000 that the project
would have owed the bank on a 6.2-metre Super Cat and two
90-horsepower outboard motors we were negotiating to buy.

This generous support changed the situation of the WSRP
from an indebted vision of hope to a fully paid-for functional
working unit, capable of setting out to sea and doing the work
with the great white sharks that was its reason for existence. Ten
days later the dream became a reality when Mazda honoured its
promise and its support of the project began.

The WSRP's first big venture came just after we had got it up
and running, when the Natal Sharks Board approached us with
a request for help in testing electronic shark barrier in the waters
off the Cape. Naturally we jumped at this opportunity, and for
six weeks assisted the NSB with extensive tests in False Bay.

The success of these tests was very limited, however, because to my great concern we encountered hardly any great whites. This was not the False Bay I knew, and I couldn't rid myself of the fear that the great whites really were on the verge of extinction. After all, I knew this bay like the back of my hand, and if I couldn't find the great whites, where had they gone? There seemed to be only one explanation: in recent years the shark hunters, like me before my turnaround, had wiped them out.

Well, it never pays to jump to a conclusion, and only a few weeks after the NSB had gone home this particular conclusion came back to bite this ten-minute shark specialist in the backside. I was talking to a commercial fisherman from Gansbaai, a small fishing village on the south coast, and he told me a very interesting tale: shark hunters there, he said, were taking out large numbers of great whites off nearby Dyer Island.

I had never heard of the big sharks congregating around Dyer Island and was sceptical about the fisherman's claim, but I called the Gansbaai harbourmaster, and what he said left me more than a little interested. The upshot of this was that on a bright October morning a few days later I checked the medium-term weather report and then set off with my team (Craig and Nico du Plooy) for the small village of Kleinbaai, approximately six nautical miles from Dyer Island.

Incidentally, 'Dyer Island' is something of a misnomer as there are actually two islands, both flat, about four kilometres from the shore and nine kilometres from where we launched our boat. Dyer Island proper, the larger of the two, is a bird colony frequented by penguins, cormorants, oyster-catchers and some other species, while on its seaward side is a smaller outcrop called Geyser Rock which houses up to 60 000 seals at certain times of the year. Separating the two is a shallow channel about 600 metres long and 150 metres wide.

Being a heavily populated bird colony, Dyer Island has a thick layer of bird droppings all over it, and several decades ago was one of the 'guano islands' off the Cape coast where labourers would spend a few months every year, collecting the smelly but valuable stuff for export. Then the guano-collecting was stopped, and the small cluster of buildings the collecting parties had used were converted for the use of an island-keeper, scientists and the odd visiting parks ranger arriving by way of a small and by now rather ramshackle jetty.

Merely launching our new 6.2-metre Super Cat was an adventure in itself. Kleinbaai's harbour was little more than a large rocky pool, and on top of that it was low tide. We were terrified of scraping the hull on the rocks after getting the boat off the trailer, and I told Craig and Nico to walk the boat towards the open sea till they were waist deep before scrambling on board.

Our concerns were not shared by the considerable crowd of locals who had gathered by now, and who found our over-protective antics highly amusing. I hope they took us a little more seriously when I opened the throttles after we had cleared the kelp beds and the Super Cat surged forward as if it were an eager racehorse.

It took us about 15 minutes to reach the leeward side of the island, and I was more than a little worried to note that the sea to both left and right was quite restless, with huge plumes of white water erupting from the shallow reefs as large waves crashed over them. I assessed the situation while we hung back in the calm of Dyer's lee and decided to avoid the dangerous-looking western side, entering the channel from the east.

Cautiously we crept up on the eastern tip of the island, only to find our way blocked by an almost solid wall of kelp that seemed to spread from the island towards the land, as far as the eye could see. I didn't like the feel of the place at all, and the kelp gave me a good excuse to call it a day and get the hell away from this hostile place without losing face with my crew. Without further ado I turned the Super Cat around and pointed the bow in the direction of the mainland.

Just as we started picking up speed, however, Craig noticed another ski boat on the other side of the kelp bed. After about eight attempts I managed to raise the boat's skipper on the radio and ask how to get through the kelp. He told me to hang on for a moment and he would show us.

This sounded like a bit of a tall story, but the other boat came skimming through the kelp as if it was running along a highway. We couldn't believe our eyes. When it came alongside the skipper explained that there was, in fact, a safe passage through the kelp, which I believed because he had just demonstrated it to me. Spirits revived, I followed him and was amazed to find that a path actually wove its way through the kelp, which had appeared impenetrable even to my expert eye.

When we were through I realised straight away that this was most definitely not a place to be taken lightly. The sea behind the island was large and very lumpy; the manner of its behaviour made you feel it was warning you of its untapped power, and it was one of those rare occasions when my customary cocky swagger found itself damped down into distinctly nervous caution.

Very carefully I negotiated the approximately 800 metres or so of open water to the mouth of the channel, but when the boat got inside it we found ourselves in a 300-metre-long stretch of dead-calm water flowing between the rocky outcrops that formed the Dyer Island channel.

This was much, much, better, and the moment I set eyes on this place, my pulse began to quicken with excitement and a sense of anticipation came over me as my shark-vibe activated itself. I just *knew* that this hostile-looking channel was great white shark territory.

Full of excitement, I instructed Nico to start chumming while I prepared my rig, exactly the same type I had used while hunting the great whites, except that the bait was now tied to the end of a rope instead of being threaded onto a hook. Craig floated the bait and its buoy out about 20 metres behind the

Super Cat, and to our amazement, only 15 minutes passed before a great white arrived and started chasing the bait, which Craig kept just out of reach of its eager jaws.

Before long a second shark made its appearance, then four more within half an hour. So within an hour we had no fewer than six great whites circling the boat, all at the same time. Holy moly! I had discovered that there was a white shark paradise on earth after all.

As we got down to our new-found trade and interacted with this mind-boggling assemblage of new acquaintances I had no doubt at all that we had discovered the white shark mecca of the world, and in the grand tradition of intrepid explorers I gave the channel a name of my own choosing: 'White Shark Alley'. It was a historic moment, and over the next three years this channel would be *the* place for top wildlife film-makers and researchers to visit and pay homage to the mighty great white shark.

On returning to Cape Town I briefed Len on our amazing discovery, which left no doubt that Dyer Island was the place where the WSRP should start its shark-tagging programme. The idea was that a tag would be inserted at the base of a target shark's dorsal fin, and when enough great whites had been tagged it would be possible to develop a database that would provide a fairly accurate population sample in due course. It was also hoped that sightings of tagged sharks would help scientists to learn more about the territorial behaviour and migration movements of great white sharks.

All we had to do was tag enough great whites to make the findings statistically significant. How many would be 'enough'? Well, that question was left open. In my own opinion, 'enough' would be the whole lot ... an impossible dream, of course, but a goal towards which to work.

SEVEN

Fame at last!

If anybody had suggested to me in the mid-1980s that there was even the remotest possibility of any government on earth considering protection laws for any predator shark species – especially the most feared one of all, the great white shark – I would have laughed out loud and told my informants that they were out of their minds even to think about it; elephants would grow wings and fly before any politician got crazy enough to try it.

Well, it's amazing, isn't it, how often loudmouths are forced to eat their words? Some months after the outing with PJ and Notch Fin, Len and I went to see the Minister of Environmental Affairs, Dr Louis Pienaar. We presented him with a proposal for the conservation of the great white shark, with the results of Nan Rice's poll included, and then left without being all that optimistic about achieving anything. But we felt some drastic action was needed because of the continuing large-scale slaughter of great whites in Cape waters; at Dyer Island alone, 17 had been caught in just one month.

A couple more months passed, and then one day in March Dr Pienaar's office called us at the museum: legislation would be introduced to protect the great white shark, a world first; the minister would make the public announcement at an international media conference at the museum the following month.

Struggling to absorb the news, Len and I summoned Mike and Craig up to the office to tell them of this astounding and unexpected development and then – the full import of Dr

Pienaar's words finally striking home – we gave ourselves over to complete elation.

Up till now the museum administration had not taken us all that seriously, but these tidings got them right behind us. Although we felt very strongly about the great whites, we hadn't expected the announcement to be as important as it turned out to be. In addition to all sorts of dignitaries, the minister's conference was attended by representatives of some major news organisations like the BBC and CNN. We were well prepared, though, and absolutely everything went like a dream.

The story exploded into the world in spite of South Africa's political isolation, and immediately our telephones and fax machines were inundated with congratulatory calls. Virtually overnight the little-known WSRP had become world-famous. We were all pretty damned proud.

Film crews from across the globe were contacting us literally within days of the announcement, and the very first group to come out and cover our work included the legendary team of Ron and Valerie Taylor. I couldn't believe that these stars of the books and the big screen were coming to South Africa to work with us. Everything seemed to be happening so fast that it was hard to take it all in.

Almost overnight, or so it felt, anyway, the WSRP stopped being a small group of enthusiasts with a very limited budget who quietly tagged sharks in between trying to educate the public about conserving them. Suddenly we were a very busy team, building big shark-filming cages and hiring boats large enough to drop them into the ocean and pull them out again without capsizing the vessel.

We didn't mind, though – not in the least. All of the hard work Craig, the others and I had put in was paying unexpected dividends, with film crews willing to pay us to work with sharks. This situation was perfect, because now our work was being recorded for the future.

Our first clients, the Taylors, arrived with a film company commissioned by National Geographic to make a documentary called *Shark Shocker*, about the electronic shark repellent that was being developed by the Natal Sharks Board, and our research and conservation efforts. It seemed that South Africa was the world leader in shark conservation at that time, and the decision to protect the great white shark had put us squarely in the limelight.

Before the Taylors arrived we all did some homework and decided to use the Dyer Island area for filming. At that stage we hadn't yet landed on the two-part island, but we had no doubts about the suitability of White Shark Alley, and so I obtained permission to stay there while filming *Shark Shocker*.

Because our operation was very much a combined effort, I asked Craig to give some of his impressions of that first film shoot of ours.

For me, it was a very exciting time and I felt really honoured to be working with these living legends of the marine world. I had seen many films with the Taylors swimming with sharks, and now I was going to be working with them. Dyer Island was just great, and beyond my expectations. I was not sure what to expect, but when we arrived out there and saw the wild action of the area, I was blown away.

It is hard to explain the feeling of the place because it really is not much to look at, but it is wild and home to birds, seals and great white sharks, so it felt as if we had found the ends of the earth.

For this shoot we used two boats, our 22-foot research boat and a converted 45-foot wooden trawler named the Gay Jane, owned by Ken Brewin, which would be our working platform for the next three weeks. My assistant, Mike Hughes, and I did all the running around with the research boat, carting provisions and equipment out to Dyer

Island and the Gay Jane, *which had anchored between the islands in White Shark Alley.*

The film trip was absolutely fantastic and we were able to tag dozens of sharks while experimenting and developing new research techniques. For me, it was an incredible opportunity to learn about wildlife filming and all the many aspects to making a successful documentary.

During this film trip we became the first people in the world to do out-of-the cage free diving with the white sharks. Spear-fishermen and the odd scuba diver had obviously been in open water with white sharks, but nobody had ever gone out there and dived with great white sharks that had been attracted to the boat with chum and baits.

Before coming down to Cape Town the Taylors had spent about a week in Durban, familiarising themselves with the electronic shark repellent developed by the Natal Sharks Board. There, Valerie got into the tank with the big bull sharks at the Durban Sea World to test the device, which seemed to work quite well. But it had to pass the white shark test, or it would be worth nothing.

At the end of the second week's filming Graeme Charter and Norman Starkey of the Natal Sharks Board arrived with their machine, called the 'Oceanic Protection Device', or just 'POD', for the make-or-break test on the great whites. They were very keen to test it, and so were we. Being a prototype, the POD was nothing to look at and pretty cumbersome, little more than a Perspex tube approximately three feet long, trailing two long cables through which the electric pulse was transmitted.

To test this device we simply attached the cables to a big chunk of seal meat at the end of a rope, bait that no self-respecting white shark would be able to resist. Norman would sit with the machine in his hand and his finger on the switch, as tense as a trigger-happy psycho with an AK-47 assault rifle, while my father stood by with the bait-line. Just before the shark took the bait in its mouth, he would shout: 'Now!' and Norman would hit the button. Almost invariably the shark would immediately swing its head away from the bait.

We made some interesting observations as testing proceeded. The closer the shark got to the bait before Norman switched on, the more vigorous its retreat would be, and after a shark had been zapped a few times it not only stayed away from the bait but gave it a wide berth.

We tested the POD for two full days, and not once did the sharks get to the bait while it was switched on. On one occasion we allowed a shark to take the bait firmly in its jaws before turning the POD on. The shark went wild when the POD's juice hit it, but it must have got some sort of lock-jaw because it couldn't let go of the bait till Norman switched off again. Then the shark spat the meat out and departed at a rate of knots, not to be seen again.

At the end of the second day we all sat down to discuss the possibility of testing the POD outside the cage. Valerie, with her steel backbone, was very keen to go free diving with the great white sharks, and Ron said that he was excited about trying, because they had never gone free diving with white sharks before.

Norman and Graeme were not too keen on this, because they felt that if anything went wrong the POD would receive very negative publicity. Being responsible for the shoot, my father had the final say on the matter, and after considering it, he said we could go for it. I asked him if I could join the dive, but he said he felt that I didn't have enough underwater experience with white sharks to risk it. I was disappointed, of course, but later I saw that he had been right to keep me back. Ron, Valerie and Mike would do the diving, along with none other than PJ, who had arrived in the channel the day before.

Typically, PJ had rolled up unannounced and uninvited, but by way of a peace-offering had brought along two barrels of fresh whale oil and some seal meat for bait, and you just can't turn away a guy with chum like that.

My father decreed that Valerie would test the POD while Ron did the filming and Mike and PJ acted as safety divers. We started chumming and soon had five big sharks around the boat. Then the divers went in. Looking back now, I realise that it bordered on the suicidal.

Later, when I started free diving with white sharks, I did so only in really good conditions, but on this day the water was so murky that visibility was down to about five metres. This meant that the sharks could approach to within a few feet before the divers were even aware of their presence, and they found themselves actually fending the sharks off with their prods.

To say this was a highly dangerous state of affairs would be putting it mildly, but all four returned safely after over half an hour later, wildly elated, and both Ron and Valerie thanked my father for allowing them to realise a dream. We were elated, too, although our elation had a lot of relief built into it. The world's first deliberate free dive with white sharks had just taken place, and our team had done it.

After the elation had subsided, my father went over to Norman to chat about the performance of the POD. He quietly told my father that the POD had leaked and shorted out, so it had been useless during the free dive.

That this sort of close interaction with sharks is dangerous goes without saying, but when I think back it's clear to me that the real danger posed by Cape waters is not the great whites but their environment, the ocean itself.

Now and again great whites will take human beings, with an inevitable furore in the media after each such incident. But the sea swallows whole ships, and often their crews, on a regular basis, and has been doing so since men first began to sail around the Cape of Good Hope. The old Portuguese navigators of the fifteenth and sixteenth centuries called it 'Cabo Tormentoso', the Cape of Storms, and they weren't exaggerating. This part of the world is notorious for its terrible storms, huge seas and hostile coastlines; at times I have found myself facing winds of up to 160 kilometres an hour and eight-metre seas – and they can go up to 14 metres.

The Cape of Storms showed its teeth on the last day of the National Geographic shoot. When the day's work was wound up Ron, Val and the film crew headed back to shore with Craig and Mike Hughes, but my wife Norma had joined me on the boat that day and had decided to stay on board the *Gay Jane* for the return trip to Gansbaai, about 20 kilometres or 16 sea miles away.

Norma was anything but a keen sailor and usually tried to avoid going to sea at all costs, but it was such a lovely afternoon that we all decided to have a light meal and then spend a little downtime relaxing in the channel before Ken Brewin took us back to Gansbaai.

We enjoyed the relaxation after our weeks of hard work, and by three o'clock we were so laid back that Ken and his girlfriend settled down in the wheelhouse for a nap and the deckhand went below for a snooze as well. Norma and I stayed on deck, stretching out on a mattress, and before too long we were also heading for dreamland.

I was pulled back to wakefulness by strange sounds that were not part of the *Gay Jane's* normal rhythm. I sat up and became aware of two alarming facts. Firstly, the anchor was dragging along the rocky bottom so fast that I could hear its chain rattling over the rocks at the bottom of the channel. Secondly, I felt a gale-force southwesterly wind blowing into my face when I raised my head above the gunwale.

I jumped up, and one quick look around us told me we were in big trouble. The wind's violent onslaught had suddenly whipped up huge seas around the island, creating a current through the channel which was powerful enough to drag the heavy anchor from its grip on the seabed. This meant that the *Gay Jane* was in real danger of grounding on the nearby rocks, and soon: they were only a few metres away.

I ran to the wheelhouse and banged on the door, bringing Ken to life. I quickly filled him in on our predicament and then ran to the bows to winch up the anchor. In the meantime Ken fired up the motor to hold the boat off the looming rocks and a rudely awakened Norma scrambled below to get the deckhand topside as quickly as possible.

A desperate five minutes or so followed while I battled to get the anchor on board and Ken kept a heavy hand on the throttles and wheel to save us from running aground. When I had eventually managed to stow the anchor I joined a visibly rattled Ken in the wheelhouse. His eyes were locked on the passage out of the channel, and I cursed under my breath when I followed his gaze and saw how ugly the sea had become. It was a wild sight, for sure, and I expect I looked as shaken as Ken when I saw what confronted us.

The sea had jacked up so much in the short time we had been asleep that constant sets of four- to six-metre waves were crashing through the narrow gap at the end of the channel, and my stomach knotted as I realised that if we wanted to escape with our lives we would have to pass head-on through this barrier of breaking water.

Not unnaturally there was an almost tangible tide of panic beginning to wash over the *Gay Jane*, and I knew that the only way to scotch it, and save our hides in the process, was to get moving. Now the experience I had gained during years of launching ski boats from the beaches of Natal paid off. Our only hope of breaking free from the massive waves holding us in the channel was to head straight into them and crash our way out ... and right away, before the rapidly deteriorating conditions made even that unpleasant option impossible.

I knew that waves usually came through in sets of three to five at a time, with a slight lull before the next set, and that would be our window of opportunity, so I told Ken to move the *Gay Jane* as close as safely possible to the Dyer Island side of the channel, and maintain position opposite the exit. Then, when I said 'go', he was to swing the boat straight into the oncoming sea and hold his course at full throttle. Clearly thinking I had lost my mind, he kept arguing that I was going to end up killing us all; the better option was to run the *Gay Jane* onto the rocks and swim for it.

I managed to convince him that there was a real danger that at least some of us would be bashed onto the rocks and drown, however, and he headed for the exit, where he had to fight to keep the *Gay Jane* in position, because the strong current and surge from the massive waves breaking nearby kept pushing us towards the rocks. Meanwhile, I studied the rhythm of the wave-sets, and when the next lull appeared, I gave Ken the 'go'.

We cleared the mouth of the channel just as the first waves of the next set started to lift their enormous heads approximately 300 metres ahead of us, and an expression of horror crossed Ken's face as he saw what we were facing. I felt pretty much the same way myself, but somehow I managed to keep a calm face, slapping him reassuringly on the back and telling him with a confidence that I didn't completely feel to just keep going and to make sure to hold a steady course.

The first wave of the new set came crashing over the bow with such crushing force that it almost washed the *Gay Jane* backwards onto Geyser Rock, which at that point was only about 30 metres astern. It was a hair-raising sight: the *Gay Jane's* deck was completely submerged as we crashed our way through the oncoming six-metre breakers. For the next 20 minutes it was touch and go before we managed to claw our way out of the island's grip.

But escaping from the channel didn't mean that we were safe. Now we would have to travel directly into an oncoming sea, which had built up to swells averaging about four metres and was getting higher all the time as the gale intensified. Soon the swells were reaching up to about six metres and breaking at their tops as they grew steeper and larger. Needless to say, our progress was pretty slow. We had managed to bash our way out of the channel just after five in the afternoon, and three hours later we had made only three and a half sea miles back towards Gansbaai, whereas under normal conditions the entire trip would have taken only about an hour and a half.

Now yet another terrible danger loomed as I sat in the wheel-house, thinking about our very slow progress. At our present rate it would be well after dark before we rounded Danger Point. This rocky headland with its ragged pinnacles of reef is notorious for killing the British troopship *Birkenhead* in the 1850s, but its reputation is not based only on that one ghastly incident; it is so lethal that all mariners treat it with the greatest respect. Even at the best of times, in daylight and a moderate sea-state, it is a dauntingly dangerous place to be.

There was no sense to upsetting the others, however, so I kept my apprehensions to myself for the time being and did no more than offer to relieve Ken at the wheel, because he was clearly taking strain as the weather and sea-state continued to deteriorate. Ken declined the offer and we struggled on for another two hours or so. Then, with huge relief, Ken blurted out that we had passed Danger Point and he could see the lights of Gansbaai in the distance. Swinging the helm hard to starboard, he brought the *Gay Jane* around to a bearing of 120 degrees.

The change of course brought an immediate improvement in our comfort, because the big racing waves were now more or less directly astern, so that the old craft lifted her head and surged forward. The mood on board suddenly changed for the better. It was as if we could feel the fear of death lifting off our weary shoulders for the first time since leaving Dyer Island.

But I could not rid myself of a feeling that something was not quite right. But what? Without saying anything that might dampen the new-found happy mood I tried to pierce the darkness with my eyes and find some specific landmark. It was almost impossible. We were enveloped in a misty haze; sheets of spray lashed the wheelhouse, and the *Gay Jane* went up and down as if we were on a giant roller coaster, alternately plunging into the deep troughs between the waves, and then rising skyward before plunging down again.

As a result I could only catch brief glimpses of the lights Ken had pointed out as Gansbaai's, and with each glimpse I became more worried. I have an acute sense of timing, and it told me that we were at least an hour short of where Ken thought we were. And the Birkenhead lighthouse seemed to be flashing too far to the west of where we were for the *Gay Jane* to be safely clear of the deadly reefs that it watched over.

I made some excuse about going on deck to check on the mooring ropes in anticipation of our arrival at Gansbaai, slid the wheelhouse door open and stepped out on deck. The wind threw an almost solid wall of saltwater spray at me that came close to knocking me off my feet. It didn't quite, and I fought my way forward, hanging on to the handrail for all I was worth while the salt water stung my eyes.

When I finally reached the bow I locked my arms around the forward stay to avoid being washed overboard and focused my attention on the patch of lights, which were now less than a kilometre away.

The raging sea was so broken up that I wasn't able to identify where we were headed till the fourth time the *Gay Jane* rose up on a wave-crest. Then a surge of cold horror that had nothing to do with the ambient temperature ran through me.

We weren't anywhere near Gansbaai. The intermittently flashing light that had raised our hopes was actually the phosphorescent glow caused by the giant waves crashing down on the dreaded Birkenhead Rock. It was like standing and looking down into our communal grave ... and at our present rate of progress the funeral service would start within a few minutes.

I scrambled back to the wheelhouse, unceremoniously shoved Ken away from the helm and started swinging the boat in as tight a 90-degree turn as I could manage. Ken, not unnaturally, protested strongly at this rough treatment, but I cut him short by telling him to open the starboard sliding window and take a good look at the lights that he had been aiming for. Swearing under his breath, he poked his head out just as the boat crested a wave broadside; less than 500 metres away the Birkenhead Rock reared up with its necklace of phosphorescence at its brightest.

Ken was so shocked that he stood next to me in stunned silence for the next ten minutes while I steered the *Gay Jane* to comparatively safer waters. When he finally found his voice he said: 'Hell, I'm sorry, I almost killed us all tonight.' There was nothing to add to that. How many sailors had died because of an understandable mistake like this, made during conditions that were almost beyond human endurance?

Two and a half hours later I managed to bring the *Gay Jane* into Gansbaai and we tied up at long last. We had got away with it! We were more fortunate than the 100-ton trawler *Prince William*, which was caught by the same storm and ran aground with some loss of life in Walker Bay, approximately 40 kilometres from Gansbaai.

Ken and I had other adventures with the *Gay Jane* before he sold her, four years and six cinematic shoots later, but never one as perilous as this, the dramatic ending to my initiation into the world of international film-making.

Anyway, after Ron and Val departed, I returned to Cape Town to catch up with the large backlog of other work that had piled up in my absence, but Graeme and Norman decided to stay behind at Dyer Island to continue testing the POD system. To this end Graeme had ordered some of his people in Durban to bring down one of the NSB netting boats with all the other equipment they wanted to test – they had now moved on to a barrier device they had built, a long electric cable designed to keep sharks away from the beaches. Graeme asked if Craig could stay behind with our research boat to assist them with the testing, and I said yes.

The testing of the beach barrier turned out to be a very interesting project for the WSRP, and once again I leave it to Craig to give a first-hand account:

I was excited, to say the least, when my father told me that I would be spending the following three weeks working with the NSB team at Dyer Island. The NSB had rented a house on shore, where we waited for a couple of days for the rest of their team to arrive. During these several days on shore, the storm in which my father had battled on the Gay Jane continued to rage, and it only subsided the evening before the NSB crew arrived.

We woke up to a calm morning with a heavy leaden sky. The wind was gone, but the sea was big, with huge lumps of grey dominating the horizon. I had a little experience of this area, but the NSB guys had just about none, so between us we were not suited to make educated calls about the sea conditions.

The plan was to take the WSRP boat, their NSB boat and a hired rigid inflatable boat (RIB) out to the island, where we would live for the duration of the testing. We piled the three boats with dive gear, shark cages, large anchors, chain, food, plenty of beer, the long steel barrier cable and other necessities. The WSRP boat was the best-suited for keeping things dry, so I ended up with the cable, two generators and the camera gear. There was only place for one boat at the jetty, and our game plan was that the other two would be winched up on arrival, while mine, which was the largest, would tie up and stay in the water.

The locals had gathered to watch all this exciting activity, and several of them asked if we were serious about going to the island in such a big sea. We said yes – the sea was big, true enough, but it was smooth, and so we figured it would be all right. But as soon as we left the little harbour and cleared the entrance my heart climbed into my throat as we got in among the gigantic swells.

All I could do was take it slowly, because my boat was very heavily laden and my companion, a cameraman named Richard Schewry, had little sea experience. So basically I was on my own in every sense of the word when the other two boats drew away from me.

The swells grew bigger and bigger as we travelled further out to sea; eventually they were so steep that my boat was broaching down their face. It was a very frightening experience, so that I was pretty shaky-handed by the time I finally reached the island, where the other two boats were already entered in the tiny anchorage. Huge rollers were drifting in, generating thunder and froth. It was not a pretty sight.

I circled out to the deep water, where the waves were not breaking, and waited for the other boats to be winched up so that I could reach the jetty. Eventually we got the signal to enter, so I carefully picked a gap and powered in. The entrance was perfectly timed, but as I got into the relative safety of the anchorage the guys on shore shouted that I had to head back out to sea. A large surge had ripped one of the boats back down the ramp, so there was no room for me while they struggled to get the situation back under control.

This was easier said than done. That terrible anchorage allowed me literally three metres of space in which to turn around. This was difficult enough in perfect conditions and pretty near impossible otherwise, and the surge was just too powerful. Before I knew it I was caught between rocks on one side and the kelp bed on the other, with absolutely nowhere to go.

Then, just to make matters even worse, a huge set of waves came barrelling in. I saw the first wave jacking up into a wall of water, sucking up the kelp as it galloped towards us. Richard was in the bow, holding on to a rope, and I shouted to him to hang on. I remember adding: 'Richard, here's big shit!'

Then the first wall of water hit us, and just as it did so I powered the boat to try to punch through it. The boat went vertical, and I ducked behind the console because I was afraid that the T-top would tear loose and smash into me. In the bow Richard was thumped brutally hard against the deck, and suddenly both engines died, having been completely submerged. Desperately, I tried to restart them as we wallowed broadside-on in the path of the next monster. No luck. Then at the last possible moment one of them came to life and I pushed the throttle forward as far as it would go.

Slowly the boat turned to meet the wave, but that was not enough. The towering pile of water smashed down on us, carrying both Richard and the equipment away with it. My only functioning motor died again, and this time I couldn't get it to restart. By now the third wave was building up. I hadn't lost my sense of self-preservation, though, so I left the controls and just before it hit the boat I somehow managed to get hold of the anchor and hurl it overboard, climbing onto the rail facing it so that I wouldn't end up under the cable if the boat capsized, which seemed very likely.

The wave hit us side on, and the boat keeled over to the point where I thought it was gone, but somehow the anchor grabbed on to a rock just long enough to pull us through the wave. There were no more waves approaching for the moment, so I quickly helped Richard back on board. We hauled up the anchor and I finally succeeded in starting the outboards; by this time the jetty was clear, so I could move in and tie up, a satisfactory ending to one of the worst experiences of my entire life.

We dived out the equipment that had been lost overboard (to our delight we hadn't lost anything that was vital to our task), and the next few weeks were both fascinating and fun. We spent every daylight hour in the channel testing the barrier, and passed the evening hours with big meals, beer and guitar music around the fire.

To test the beach barrier we ran the cable out from the island in a 15-metre arch, stationing one boat inside, another at the end of the cable with the generator and the third just on the outside of the cable. All three boats would chum non-stop all day to attract sharks, and we switched the cable on and off for alternating two-hour periods, monitoring their behaviour at all times.

We found that when the current was off the sharks would approach the boat without hesitation to take the baits, but when it was on they stayed well away. Not once did the sharks try to take any of the baits while the current was on. So there was no doubt that the barrier was working.

In the last week of testing we also provided the Natalians with a good war story to take back when we had a very exciting but frightening encounter with a huge great white. We had run low on bait and decided to put one of the guys ashore on Geyser Rock to see if there were any dead seals lying around that we could press into service.

Early one morning, before starting work on the barrier-testing, we set off to land the designated carcass-scout, Paul van Blerk. The channel was very calm, and so all three boats idled up the seal colony to find a good spot for Paul to land from the RIB. The NSB men had promised the owner of the RIB that they would return it undamaged, so its skipper hove to a couple of metres from the rocks and Paul slipped off the bow onto a waist-deep ledge, from which he slowly climbed out of the water.

Right in front of him was a large bull seal with his harem of about five females. The seals obviously did not like the look of Paul, because they slid right past him and dived into the water. The bull seal surfaced about two metres behind Paul and turned to look back at him. Then the seal's head snapped back as a huge great white shark, easily five metres long, appeared out of nowhere and slammed into it.

The momentum drove the seal onto the ledge just below Paul's feet for a second before the shark dragged it away again and tore it to pieces in spectacularly violent and gory fashion. We watched, fascinated by such a display of brute power almost within touching distance.

Except Paul, of course, who was not fascinated but shocked to the core, seeing that mere seconds earlier he had been standing in the water where the bull seal had been turned into lunch. When he got back to the water's edge after his search the RIB had to creep right up to the rocks, damage or no damage, to allow Paul to climb on board without getting his feet wet. I can't say I blame him.

EIGHT

One inch from death

Cage diving has come a long way since its early days, although even now most people's reaction to the idea of going down in a cage to view great white sharks is, 'You have to be out of your mind,' and this upgrades itself to 'You're totally insane!' when they see our more recently developed cages.

Gone are the days of gorilla cages, requiring heavy lifting equipment and large boats. The ones we use today are small and constructed of material not very different from that used to make a parakeet's cage, which any white shark with a mean disposition could quite easily turn into mangled scrap metal.

But it doesn't happen. Our shark cages aren't wrappings around candy bars. A shark doesn't look at the steel wrapping around the human in the cage and then decide to get inside for a taste of rubber-clad finger food. That is the conclusion we reached fairly early on as we started to understand shark psychology, and after repeated cage dives, almost certainly more than anyone else's, nothing has happened to change our minds.

Perspectives are quite different when you are looking at the matter from the shark's point of view. Humans have a tendency to think that all creatures look at things the way they do. Thus it is clear that the shark knows we are in the cage and will tear it open to get at us. But does the shark necessarily see matters the same way?

When a shark is swimming around the cage, it knows that there is something alive inside. It can see movement, smell us and detect our respiration and heart beat, but can it distinguish between the cage and the contents of the cage? I believe that the sharks see the cage and the human in it as one object and when they come to investigate, they taste the inedible steel of the cage and back off. Is there any reason why they should think that the diver would taste any better than the cage?

Many people are surprised that we have never yet had a white shark attack one of our cages, although we have had them accidentally enter the camera port on two different occasions. Our rare hair-raising close encounters with great whites have always been due to human error, not the result of evil intentions on the part of the sharks concerned.

This is not to say that the learning curve has always been a gentle gradient, or even a safe one at times. When diving with great whites became popular and the cage-diving requests started rolling in we decided that we would use every media opportunity that came along to promote sharks as the important animals they were, so most of the time we said 'yes', and each time took on a huge responsibility.

Shark cages, underwater cameras, crazy cameramen and out-of-their-depth directors (in both senses of the word): all these guys looked to us as the experts, but the truth was that we were on a crash course of discovery ourselves. Needless to say, we had some very close calls, and each time my heart would be in my throat as I thought of the possible repercussions, media and otherwise, if someone was savaged or taken out altogether. But somehow we always got away with it.

I remember one of the early trips. The clients were Thomas Horton and Associates, who wanted to feature our work in a shoot they were doing for the Discovery Channel called *African Shark Safari*. They were a bunch of nice Americans with whom we got on well from the start; Wes Skyles, their chief underwater cameraman, was a real character in addition to being a very likeable chap.

Wes seemed to be quite fearless, and impressed everybody with his daring and aggressive style of camera work. We were all convinced that his footage would form a vital part of the movie. Alas, life is full of disappointments. Three days after his first nine reels of film were rushed off to the United States for processing and evaluation, the film's director, Thomas Horton, got a shirty call from the studio. All nine reels were blank. Was this some form of practical joke?

It was not. Wes was using a new type of underwater camera he had developed, and investigation showed that he had been feeding in the film the wrong way around. The poor guy was absolutely devastated by this highly embarrassing and costly mistake, and in the ensuing days we discovered that Wes seemed to have a talent for attracting trouble of one kind or another. He was, as the saying goes, an accident looking for a place to happen: if there was any sort of mishap or drama on board, you could be sure that Wes would be right in the middle of it, and most often the actual cause of it.

As an example: for some inexplicable reason the white sharks completely disappeared from the channel for nine days during the second week of the shoot. Wes became bored with sitting around and decided to visit the seal colony on Geyser Rock. Our walking disaster landed without mishap, but then he spotted a seal pup that was not more than three weeks old, and things began to go wrong almost immediately.

Wes realised that his new acquaintance could provide an interesting shot for the film. He attracted the attention of the film crew on the *Gay Jane* close by and instructed them to start the camera rolling, then went through the motions of discovering the infant among the rocks, scooping up the tiny little thing and holding it close to his chest like a father holding a baby.

It was really touching stuff and stole the hearts of everybody concerned except the seal pup, which took exception to the proceedings and bit Wes on the cheek. Wes instantly put the pup down where he had found it and started making his way back to the boat in fairly dignified haste, which soon turned into something a little more active when he passed too close to a large bull seal. The seal reared up and bit him on the shoulder, and Wes's retreat turned into a mad dash for the boat.

In all fairness, though, Wes didn't lose his laid-back Californian sense of humour. 'Well, fellows,' he said as he climbed back on the *Gay Jane*, 'that's one to mankind and two to the seals.'

A few days later the white sharks returned to the channel with a vengeance and Wes was back in the shark cage, happily doing his underwater thing. On that particular morning there were four white sharks near the boat, ranging in size from about 3.5 metres to 4.5 metres long, and we all knew that Wes was having a great time filming them as they cruised in on the cage from all angles, sometimes to within inches of the camera ports.

Topside, Craig was also having a ball as he encouraged the white sharks to visit the cage by dragging the baits away from them towards the cage, bringing them so close that occasionally they actually bumped against it. This was all very well, but then things hotted up to an alarming degree. A 3.5-metre male came swimming straight at the cage in hot pursuit of the bait, so intent on what it was doing that it did not realise till the last moment that it was about to collide with the stern of the boat.

The shark took immediate evasive action, but it had become confused and instead of swinging left to avoid the cage it turned right and smashed into it with great force. The shark's snout bored into the camera port, hitting Wes's camera and knocking him off balance; then the momentum of its 700-kilo body rammed its head in even deeper. The shark's tail began to lash wildly, driving it even deeper into the cage; the camera port's bars bent open and suddenly the great white was *inside* the cage with Wes, with only its tail still sticking out.

Horror-stricken, I stood on the dive platform and watched helplessly as Wes engaged in a life-and-death struggle with the shark. All he could do was stay as far as possible from the struggling shark's lethal jaws, no easy task in the cramped confines of the cage. It became even less easy when the camera port opened some more and virtually the entire shark was inside the cage. Talk about an underwater cameraman's worst nightmare.

Wes dropped to his knees and then, when even more of the shark squeezed in, dropped to the bottom and took up a foetal position, fending off the intruder's razor teeth with his camera. But it was a feeble defence. If the highly stressed and desperate shark got a grip anywhere on Wes's body it wouldn't let go but almost certainly rip him to pieces.

Then I snapped out of my trance. No blood was flowing from the cage yet, which meant that there was still a slim chance of saving him from death. I screamed at Craig and Mike to grab the cage's rope and pull it in. They hauled with all their strength and very soon the cage was close enough for me to grab the shark's protruding tail. I started pulling on it as hard as I could. I was pretty strong, but all that happened was that the shark starting jerking my 120-kilo frame around like a feather.

I hung on with every ounce of determination I had in my body, but already I could feel my strength starting to fail, and knew that I would only be able to hang on for a few seconds more. I dropped to my backside on the dive platform, placed my feet firmly on the rim of the cage's roof to gain some sound leverage and threw everything I had into one final effort. Then, through my exhaustion, I felt a flash of excitement when my legs began to straighten as I pulled the shark out, inch by inch.

I had managed to dislodge about two-thirds of the thrashing body free from the cage when a new opportunity presented itself – a pretty slim one, but better than nothing. The frantic shark jammed its head into the camera opening on the other side of the cage, then started shifting from side to side to get free of this new constriction. I pushed and kicked him *forward* with all that remained of my strength, and to my joy it worked.

With my ungentle assistance the shark's head and body were driven through the camera port. It twisted and rolled violently, and then it was all the way through and rushing off in a plume of spray. Moments later Wes popped out of the entry hatch at the top of the sadly bent and buckled cage, eyes as big as tennis balls behind the glass of his mask.

And grinning like a lunatic, the mad bastard.

'Oh, my God, that was awesome!' he blurted, 'That mean motherfucker was trying to eat my goddamn camera, oh, man, that was great!'

We stared at him speechlessly, hard put to it to believe what our ears were telling us. Minutes before, this sawn-off little runt had, literally, been snatched from the jaws of death, and instead of having a slight fit of the shakes like any reasonable man would, he was acting like a kid who had just had his first roller-coaster ride and couldn't wait to tell the world about how exciting it had been.

The Arabs have a saying that lunatics are beloved of God, and no doubt that applies to lunatic cameramen as well. Wes not only emerged from this close encounter of the worst kind without a scratch, but had kept his movie camera rolling the whole time, getting the entire episode in dramatic close-up.

Craig, meanwhile, had been developing his own theories about suitable shark cages, but I didn't realise this till the afternoon I turned into my driveway after a day's work on the white shark display at the V&A Waterfront and caught sight of Craig and Chris Fellows working on something.

As I drew closer I saw that it vaguely resembled a shark cage, although the flimsy contraption that they were building was most definitely far too weak for any such purpose, and concluded that they were knocking it together for the Waterfront display.

I was soon disillusioned. Craig interrupted my progress to the comfort of my well-stuffed lounge chair by calling me over to have a look at the contraption they were building. It was a shark cage, he said, and they planned to use it on our very next trip out to Dyer Island. My immediate response to this bit of news was a helpful: 'You have got be out of your bloody mind if you think I'm going to allow you to dive with any sharks in that piece of shit!'

This might seem a somewhat extreme response, but the so-called cage didn't inspire any confidence at all. It was made up of 12-millimetre aluminium tubing, bound together with plastic electrical harness straps. In fact it was so flimsy that it actually wobbled around if anyone touched it, and leaned over like the tower of Pisa when left to stand on its own. All my instincts told me that this alleged shark cage was, without any doubt, an accident looking for a place to happen.

For the next two days Craig and Chris tried to convince me that their cage would do the job, but all I could see was the bars of the cage sticking out like toothpicks on either side of a white shark's jaw, with the diver's legs and flippers protruding from the middle like a forked tongue. Eventually Craig got so tense about it that he accused me of being jealous of his creation and scared that my cage design would not match up to his.

Taking the bait he had thrown at me – I should have known better – I told him he could do what the hell he pleased with his dumb-arsed excuse for a cage, but there was no way I would in-volve myself with his harebrained scheme. If he wanted to have his nuts chewed off by a white shark, he was welcome to go out there with Chris and play Russian roulette, but since I had no desire to involve myself in their suicide attempt, I would not let him lower his death trap into the water in my presence.

That was more or less what he wanted, of course, and a few weeks later he got his opportunity to play touch-and-go with a white shark's digestive system when he, Chris and a friend called Rob were working at Dyer Island on their own.

What happened is something best told by Craig himself:

It was just after eight o'clock in the morning when we arrived at the Dyer Island channel and dropped anchor. A good day at Dyer was when a moderate southeasterly wind was blowing and there was a one-metre swell with ten metres' visibility, and on this particular day, 27 August 1992, the conditions were absolutely perfect.

The wind was light and variable from the north, there was no swell and the visibility was at least 20 metres. This unbelievable weather pattern was in the middle of August, right in the heart of our winter, when the big anti-cyclones rolling in from the cold southern ocean usually bring heavy rains, high winds and huge swells.

Thanks to the great winter storms we had been confined to land for almost two months, and were very excited at being on the water again, especially in such unexpectedly perfect conditions. Before the boat had even pulled tight on the anchor rope, Rob, Chris and I enthusiastically jumped to our routine of rigging up for white sharks. As I pounded away at the sardines in the chum-drum with a mashing pole, Chris spoke for all of us when he said: 'I really hope we get sharks today.'

None of us knew that that we were going to get our wish, doubled and with bells on, so that the next two days would turn out to be the best white shark diving ever experienced in the world, and also the most frightening.

At the Cape of Good Hope, the months of June, July and August always bring such adverse weather conditions that you are lucky to get to sea more than a few days a month. Those stand-by days were used for working on research data, maintaining equipment and designing or building new types of field equipment.

We had spent the last few weeks constructing an ultra-light shark cage; our existing cages were made of steel, and although they were built to be light, my aim had been to cut almost 50 per cent of the weight by using the same design but substituting aluminium for the steel. We succeeded pretty well – when we had finished building the cage it was so light that one man could easily lift it. So we stuck it on the boat and waited for the weather to clear so that we could test it. And now the moment had come.

We had no bait in the water yet and Chris was still mashing the chum when the first shark arrived. We were excited, to say the least, and it took only about a minute of feverish activity to get one of the baits tied to a rope and in the water. It was the start of a glorious day, a riot of shark sightings, no less than 18, and the best cage diving.

Chris and I took it in turns to spend time taking photographs and recording markings and sex in our superlightweight aluminium cage, and we were busy all the time – there wasn't a second during the entire day when there wasn't at least one shark around the boat. The sharks were very calm, and although they readily approached the cage, they didn't try to bite or mouth it.

Two of the sharks were absolutely enormous at almost five metres each, and one of them kept swimming right beneath the cage, so that its huge dorsal fin sometimes touched the bottom. When that happened it was just as if you were standing on its back (which, incidentally, was quite a bit wider than the cage itself).

We left Dyer Island that afternoon with our minds blown away. We had been off the water for weeks and would have been happy to see one shark, but instead we had seen 18 of them in almost crystal-clear water. The next morning we were in the channel at the crack of dawn with our baits tied to ropes and our chum already mashed up; we didn't want to waste even one minute of the day on anything other than white sharks. It sounds unlikely, but the conditions seemed to be even better than they had been the day before.

We anchored in the same spot and immediately put the baits in the water. Rob and I unstrapped the cage and deployed it while Chris started ladling chum into the water with great enthusiasm, and only five minutes later we had our first shark. Just 15 minutes after that we had sighted another three. Wall-to-wall sharks for the second day running! It was incredible.

I decided to go into the cage first, so I squeezed into my wetsuit while Rob and Chris played an exhausting game of tug-of-war with a couple of very big opponents. Although it is very hard work holding on to a rope with an 800-kilo great white shark rolling and thrashing about at the other end, it is also an incredible adrenaline rush and one that tends to leave you with the shakes because it has burnt up all your blood sugar.

To the uneducated eye this might have appeared to be sheer taunting, but we have good reasons for trying to keep the bait away from the sharks. Firstly, these are truly wild creatures, so we do not want to feed them as if they were domestic pets. This is also why we use their natural food, like seal or whale meat, which we get from the mammal research people, and which is hard to come by at times. Secondly, if a shark takes several pieces of bait there is a good chance that it will leave the area full and satisfied.

The sharks were much more active than the day before, and Chris and Rob had their work cut out to prevent the bait from being grabbed off the ropes.

Soon I was suited up, and attaching dive cylinders to my backpack. Normally this would be the job of whoever was not diving, but on this day the sharks were cooking and the others were too busy to help me. I didn't mind because I prefer to rig up my own equipment, but there was so much loud, excited shouting from Chris and Rob that I found myself battling to concentrate.

They certainly had enough to shout about. White sharks are always very impressive, and they are even more so when they are circling your boat from only metres away and sometimes even bumping against the hull as they arrow in towards the bait. Under such circumstances even a grown man tends to act like a child at a fireworks display.

Now Rob managed to find the time to give me a hand with the cylinders and the two weight-belts for my waist – in cage diving we always use more than double our weight to keep us stable and lessen the chances of being banged around by the surging water. Film documentaries always make it look comfortable in the cage, but in reality, you usually get bashed and tugged around by the current to at least some extent. The water was very calm on this day, though, with almost no swell or current, and promised a relatively comfortable cage session.

Chris reluctantly pulled in the baits – he was still as high as a kite on adrenaline, like the rest of us – while Rob and I manipulated the cage into a safe entry position astern. I sat down on the transom and let my legs hang down into the cage opening, then heaved myself forward and dropped in. Having settled myself into a more or less comfortable position I began orientating myself – I was facing downstream from the boat – and looking around for the sharks.

The water was crystal clear, and some distance away I could see a young male shark of around 2.8 metres long approaching from my right. He homed in on the cage, then turned gently away when he was approximately three metres from it and went past. But he was interested, and when he was about a body length away he turned around on his axis and came back.

I moved up close to the camera port in case I had an opportunity to touch him as he brushed past or mouthed the bars. One of my greatest pleasures is touching a white shark *with my bare hands – the sensation as your hand slides along the muscled flank of one of these massive creatures is indescribable. I had already calculated the shark's likely course and positioned myself to stroke his flank when he suddenly changed direction and, with several powerful tail-strokes, disappeared beyond the parameters of my field of vision.*

I realised immediately what had happened: there was a new, bigger boy on the block, and in characteristic white shark fashion the smaller one had moved off at top speed. I looked to the left to see how much bigger the new arrival was. It was big, definitely over four metres long; no wonder the first one had made tracks.

By the time an hour had passed I had identified no fewer than eight individual sharks that were cruising constantly around the cage. Three of them were particularly interested in the cage, to the point where I had to whack one or other of them on the snout with my camera on several occasions. This did not frighten them but it was enough to make them change course in most cases.

Another 15 sharks later I decided to go topside and start recording my observations. I flipped up the cage lid up and surfaced with the top of my body protruding from the opening. Then I steadied myself, found some footing on the bars on the inside of the cage and lifted my body about a third out of the water before taking the regulator out of my mouth to ask Chris and Rob to haul me up.

What I didn't realise was that the new cage was not as buoyant as a standard one, and that when I lifted myself above the surface, the front of the cage, the part on which my buttocks were resting, was almost a foot underwater. Rob began hauling the cage back to the boat with me still partly inside, excitedly telling them about what I had seen below. Then suddenly both Chris and Rob shouted 'Drop into the cage!' in perfect sync.

I *didn't ask questions or even replace my regulator, just let go and fell straight inside, looking around as I went down to see a large white shark with its head and jaws above the surface, homing in on the area my backside had occupied moments before. With my weight off the cage it bobbed back to its designed position and obstructed the shark's approach. The shark turned away and disappeared into the gloom, while I sat crouching on the bottom of the cage collecting my senses. When I went up again I didn't try anything fancy, just stuck my head out and asked to be pulled in.*

We went over what had happened and agreed that the sharks were definitely acting rather strangely and more aggressively than the day before. Now it was Chris's turn, and I advised him to be careful, because the sharks had mouthed the cage with a little more enthusiasm than was comfortable on several occasions while I was underwater. The cautionary words didn't slow him down, and before I had even stripped down and changed into a dry T-shirt and shorts, he had kitted up and got into the water.

The cage slowly drifted downstream of the boat, and before the tether-line had even been pulled taut, Chris had two sharks for company. He got to work right away, and through the clear, calm water we could see him firing away with the stills camera. After about ten minutes, the jitters from my close encounter had subsided, and Rob and I fell back into our normal observation routine. More sharks had started arriving in the interim, and we could see that they were definitely more interested in the cage and what was inside it than they had been the day before, so that Chris had to ward off the more inquisitive ones with the camera.

By this time there were more than a dozen sharks around the boat and cage, and several times two sharks would approach the cage simultaneously from opposite directions. One female of about 3.2 metres long repeatedly came back to stick her snout into the viewing port as if asking to be photographed, and Chris was happy to oblige, so happy that his guard began to slip. At each pass he let her get closer and further into the opening before taking evasive action.

Chris had now been down for almost half an hour, and in that time there was not one second in which he had not seen at least one shark. I started contemplating my second cage dive for the day, because such exceptionally warm, stable conditions were not common, and the sharks were so active around the baits that we pulled one out of the water and took turns manipulating the rope with the other one.

The female was still making frequent trips to the cage and nudging it, and now she came in from the starboard side of the boat and swam between the cage and the boat, then turned downstream and went off slightly to the left of the cage. When she was about eight metres out she turned again and headed back to the cage, slowly approaching it head-on before gently veering off to the left as she closed the gap. There was nothing unusual about her behaviour. White sharks usually develop a repetitive swimming pattern around the boat and cage when nothing happens to them on their first few passes.

Mouth slightly agape, the shark covered the remaining two metres or so, her nose directly in line with the camera port, and bumped the cage just above the port opening. Normally a shark backs off at this point, but she stayed there, almost motionless, as her nose came down ten centimetres and entered the port. Rob and I expected Chris to give her a whack with the camera at this point, but he did not, and she came even further into the cage.

Then it happened. She closed her mouth slightly, which made her more streamlined and allowed her to slip an extra few centimetres further in till her head jammed in the port, although she wasn't seriously trapped. But when she tried to open her mouth again and failed she started to become panicky, swinging her body around as she tried to back away. The cage was off-centre, however, and instead of backing out of it, she slid further in.

Now the cage had a hold on her, preventing a retreat, and the shark exploded into full-blown panic, the result of which was that she became even more firmly stuck in this alien object, the object that not only held her but had also locked her jaws closed. She started rolling and thrashing around with such vigour that the cage was dragged through the water at a precarious angle while Rob and I watched with growing concern.

I wasn't totally worried yet, because although we could make out exactly what was going on just below the surface I knew that the camera port was too small for the shark to slip through entirely. The chances were that she would eventually free herself and swim off. What we didn't know was that the top port rail was badly designed, and that the shark was exerting a lot of pressure on this design flaw with her powerful thrashing.

After a few seconds of this – although it seemed much longer at the time – the top rail suddenly bent and snapped. The light aluminium mesh above the port simply folded upwards like foil under the shark's onslaught, and what had been 40-centimetre gap turned into a gaping hole in the top of the cage. Next moment the shark was in the cage with Chris, and I became really scared. The great white shark is the most lethal wild creature on this planet, and here our friend and colleague was trapped in a cage with one.

This was truly a nightmare, and I stood there with my heart pounding while Rob said, over and over: 'No, oh, my God, no.' We knew that Chris was going to die a horrible death right in front of our eyes, because the shark was wild with fear by now, twisting and thrashing about with all its *might. Pieces of the cage broke loose and were cast aside like broken plastic; two of the buoyancy floats had already gone, so that the additional weight of the shark pulled the cage below the surface. As it sank, the shark, now fully submerged, gained extra traction and leverage (we couldn't see it from where we stood, but the shark was actually starting to bend the cage's bars outward).*

All this had distracted our attention from the other sharks, but now we were abruptly reminded of them as a large specimen began circling the cage. This represented an additional serious danger, because this shark, or even one of the others, could become excited by the frenzied activities of Chris's unwanted companion and attack her. Even if Chris somehow managed to escape from the cage when this happened he would most certainly be confronted by several other overexcited sharks.

There was another possibility, which was just as bad. By great good fortune the tether-line was attached to a section of the cage that the female had not destroyed so far, but it was not impossible that she might still tear the cage loose and swim off with it, with Chris trapped inside and condemned to certain death.

Rob and I started hauling the cage towards the boat with every ounce of adrenaline-fed strength that we could muster, hoping like hell that Chris was still in one piece. In point of fact he was, although that was a situation that could change at any second. He was huddled on the floor of the cage, unable to do anything to help himself except ward off the highly stressed shark by pushing at her belly to keep her gnashing jaws away from his legs and body. What really saved Chris's life that day was that he kept a cool head in spite of the incredible danger, knowing that if he panicked he would die, and knowing, too, that Rob and I would be busting our guts to get him back safely.

We managed to get the cage up alongside the boat and had a moment's respite. The shark's tail was now clear of the water, which meant that her destructive potential was sharply reduced, and on top of that she went into a form of static shock as a result of the huge stress she had suffered. We knew it would not last long, but in this situation a few seconds were all that was needed to make a life-or-death difference, and we made use of every one of them.

We literally grabbed the opportunity by the tail and heaved the shark backwards out of the cage. It rolled free of the mangled wreck and made off at top speed. Immediately afterwards a wild-eyed Chris emerged from the shambles like a rocket, so shaken that it was a good ten minutes before he could give us a coherent account of his misadventures.

Looking back on this, all I can do is thank Heaven that we didn't lose Chris that day – I remember that I shuddered at the thought of how I would face the almost impossible tasking of breaking the news of his death to his mom. The bottom line is that we were very lucky indeed to get away with nothing more serious than a wrecked cage, a seriously rattled shark and an even more rattled crew.

We could have ended up with a dead or badly injured diver and a flood of worldwide publicity about what would inevitably have been portrayed as a shark attack, even though the shark concerned had not been guilty of anything more than a case of too much curiosity. In a nutshell, it could have been Jaws time all over again, and never mind the fact that the whole thing had resulted from a combination of bad design and unforeseen circumstances.

I could just imagine how this would have been presented if there had been a film crew on board. Inevitably there would have been footage of our struggle to get Chris back on board, and then shots of him describing his harrowing encounter *next to the wrecked cage. That would have been fine if we were a bunch of gung ho shark-dive operators who wanted to make headlines, even if it took the story completely out of context, except that we weren't.*

Unfortunately sharks always get a bad press. Many people want to believe that they are evil cage-wrecking man-eaters, and so it is very easy for the unscrupulous to capitalise on this morbid fascination. Yet our close encounter was of our own making, and the shark was simply an innocent victim which had been sucked into a completely alien situation.

I have no doubt that Craig learned his lesson that day. As I noted earlier in this chapter, we have had close encounters with white sharks but have never had one of our cages deliberately attacked by a white shark. The scene in *Jaws* in which the shark smashes open the bars of the cage in its relentless pursuit of the diver is pure fiction. Scenes in documentary films depicting white sharks attacking cages are set-ups – bait is attached to the cage, out of camera-shot; when the sharks come into feed on it they become confused by the electrical fields emitted by the steel and end up biting the cages. In other cases, bait is dragged past the cage, away from the pursuing sharks, and after being repeatedly teased in this manner the sharks eventually vent their frustration by biting the cage.

The truth of the matter is that the sharks in such scenes are not trying to eat the cage or get at the diver inside it. All they are doing is reacting to a situation that has been created by their interaction with humankind.

NINE

Film adventures and misadventures

About a year and three documentary films after the Taylor shoot, a French film producer named Xavier arrived in South Africa with a two-man crew to work with the WSRP. The idea was to work on a white shark behavioural wildlife shoot, but what I didn't realise was that I would also get a crash course on film producers' behaviour.

We arranged for Ken Brewin and the *Gay Jane* to be waiting for us in the Dyer Island channel, and on a perfect February summer's morning we ferried them out there in the WSRP boat. They transferred their equipment to the *Gay Jane*. As they came aboard, I introduced them to White Shark Alley, and within 20 minutes the chum slick, on which Ken's crew had been working for the past two hours, had attracted no fewer than four great white sharks.

This willingness to cooperate had the Frenchmen in high spirits and smiling from ear to ear, but it didn't give them the itch for immediate action that always gripped me at such time, and a full hour later they still hadn't set up their kit to start filming.

I asked Xavier when they would be ready, and to my surprise he replied: 'Theo, we have paid for and hired the WSRP's services for two weeks, and I am confident that there is plenty of time for me to get started.' I was a bit stung by his manner but I walked away from it, thinking: *Well, Mr Big Shot, if you want to waste your time and money, then it's your baby.* All I knew was that you didn't waste such perfect conditions, because you had no control over them.

Previous page and above: Throughout my years as a shark hunter and later as a conservationist, I never experienced an unprovoked attack on a boat. As aggressive as they may appear, the sharks in these photographs have been lured to the boat by baited lines.

The dark days of white shark hunting: a juvenile white shark is stranded on the beach (top left); I pose with one of the 28 sharks I killed during my time as a hunter (top right); I proudly show off what my terminal traces looked like (above); and I pose for the media after one of my kills (right). Fortunately, these days are long gone.

Above and below: White sharks are encouraged to approach boats by researchers and tour operators, who drag hookless bait ropes through the water.

A *white shark (right) takes a baited line with no hook.*

A *life and death struggle (below) erupts when a white shark accidentally enters the camera port on the cage from which cameraman Wes Skyles is filming underwater.*

The glory days of the White Shark Research Project: I admire the research boat funded by the Mazda Wildlife Fund (top); Gerhard Visser hands over the new research vehicle (left); and one of the white shark tags used by the research project (above).

This massive white shark is about to be tagged from the safety of the research vessel.

My son Craig poses with a dead mako brought in by fishermen so that we could dissect it for research purposes.

This disturbing image is from a poster depicting humankind's intolerance and inexplicable destruction of sharks.

Creature of contrasts: A shark can brutally destroy a seal in seconds ...

... yet it is also able to calmly take bait presented from the safety of a boat.

Mean or misunderstood?

Xavier discovered that, too. About three more hours passed before the team's cameraman, Rock Pascedere, was rigged and inside the cage. He spent the next half-hour or so shooting about four minutes' worth of film, and then the sharks disappeared without any warning. And not only did they disappear, they stayed away. Eventually this got Xavier quite agitated, and his casual manner of a little earlier turned into a barrage of questions as to why the sharks had suddenly disappeared.

I found this sudden switch quite comical, although at first I had difficulty satisfying his sudden anxiety because I was also bewildered by the sudden disappearance. Then, after about two hours, a strong southwesterly started blowing, and I realised that a storm was brewing and that the sharks must have sensed the imminent change in the weather. With the memory of our near-fatal experience after the Taylor shoot the previous year still vivid in my memory, I told Ken right away to up-anchor and head for Gansbaai, from where I would run the film crew back to Kleinbaai in the WSRP boat.

The Frenchmen couldn't understand the urgency of our departure, and as we slowly made our way to the exit side of the channel Xavier demanded an explanation. I explained how unpredictable and dangerous this stretch of coast could be when a storm came out of the west. He looked distinctly sceptical, but by the time we had rounded the island and entered the pathway through the kelp bed the sea was already looking pretty ugly.

I have to admit that I enjoyed seeing the sudden expressions of concern and surprise spreading over the Frenchmen's faces when they saw the swells jacking up to about three metres, and then the angry sea that abruptly confronted us as we came out from behind the sheltered leeward side of the island. Serve them bloody right to be so contemptuous about my decision.

We saw the *Gay Jane* off to Gansbaai and then set off to Kleinbaai in our own boat. It wasn't a pleasant trip. We had to hang on for dear life as we bashed our way through growing swells that were rapidly turning into large breaking waves. The sea was really cooking as we neared the tiny harbour, and I noticed that the entrance was being closed off by large breakers crashing onto the rocks that protected the harbour.

To avoid the large kelp bed in front of the harbour I would have to run in broadside-on to these waves, and if my timing on the final dash inside wasn't absolutely perfect the boat would almost certainly capsize and the whole lot of us would be smashed against some very jagged rocks. I throttled back, bringing the boat to a violently bobbing crawl about 800 metres from the harbour entrance. Fighting to keep it under control, I studied the unpleasant situation ahead and tried to gauge the right moment; we would have just one shot, and the slightest error in judgement would bring disaster.

We spent the next 20 minutes or so being tossed around while I waited for a suitable gap between the massive waves that came galloping past and crashing like a clap of thunder onto the rocks. Then I spotted the gap between two sets of waves that I had been waiting for. Immediately I slammed both throttles wide open. The boat leapt forward like a startled rabbit and we raced towards the harbour entrance at top speed. Kleinbaai, here we came.

The tiny harbour entrance was rapidly drawing closer when the sea introduced a new buggeration factor. A really large wave jacked up less than 200 metres behind us and started catching up on us at an alarming rate: definitely very bad news, because we would soon have to turn broadside-on to get past the kelp bed. There would be no second-prize winner in this race, I knew, cold fear in my heart. Either we outran our pursuer or we were dead ducks. I squeezed the very last bit of power out of the howling outboards and slid through into the harbour literally seconds before the monster wave raced past the entrance and spent itself on the rocks with a thunderous roar.

I didn't actually go down on my knees and kiss the ground, but it was one of only two occasions in my not uneventful life on which I was so relieved to make it to safety that I actually felt like laughing and crying simultaneously. It had been that close.

As soon as we had hauled the boat from the water I rushed around to Gansbaai to await the *Gay Jane's* arrival, and I was mightily relieved when I saw her round Danger Point and steam into the bay some 20 minutes later. As soon as Ken had tied up at her moorings we lashed down everything on board in preparation for what was obviously going to be one hell of a storm.

Which it was. It raged for two full days, with the sea piling up into giant eight-metre waves that could clearly be heard crashing like distant thunder onto the reefs surrounding Dyer Island, some nine kilometres away.

On the morning of the third day the storm was gone and had been replaced by a typical warm, windless Cape summer's day. This didn't help much, though, because the storm had agitated the sea so far out that the waves had actually grown bigger instead of subsiding.

The fourth day brought little improvement; the waves were still pumping through at a height of more than six metres, which was much what it had been like when we had made our death-defying dash into the Kleinbaai harbour four days earlier.

Realising how hopeless the situation was, I told Xavier that there was no way we could put to sea. Xavier wasn't happy with this. In his opinion the sea was not so rough that it was necessary to postpone the shoot for another day. I understood his frustration, but I repeated that it would be almost impossible to leave the Kleinbaai harbour, let alone get anywhere near the Dyer Island channel. But Xavier was having none of this.

'Theo,' he said, 'I have sailed for many years and I have experienced far rougher conditions with no harm or danger to me or my crew.' I stuck to my opinion, we argued some more and then he suggested – with Rock in full agreement, although not the third man – that perhaps I was too scared to take them to the island.

That was it! I should have treated Xavier's remarks with the contempt they deserved, but this snide attack on my courage and seamanship filled me with such anger that I came close to punching this arsehole into the middle of next week. The consequence was that I swallowed Xavier's bait like a dimwitted mackerel and allowed my stubborn pride and inflated opinion of myself to overrule my common sense. There was no way on God's earth that this big-mouthed Frenchman was going to tell me that I was a coward. I would make these bastards eat humble pie before the day was over.

So instead of punching his lights out I got myself under control and, in a voice frosty enough to make a polar bear shiver, told him to get his equipment and his arse onto the boat. The Frenchmen started scrambling on board, happy in their ignorance of what awaited them, but Craig and Liam Reynolds told me bluntly that it was crazy to attempt putting out to sea in such dangerous conditions and flatly refused to follow them.

By now I had calmed down and knew they were right, and I was on the point of agreeing with Craig and calling it a day when I noticed Xavier speaking to his mates in French and making it very obvious that they disagreed with us. I was overtaken once more by my stupid pride and decided to go ahead, taking only Xavier and Rock with me and leaving the more sensible third Frenchman behind.

I posted Craig and Chris on a rocky outcrop at the harbour entrance to give me a signal the moment there was a lull between the sets of monster waves pounding the coast; from where I was I couldn't see anything, so my very life would depend on Craig's judgment. But I trusted him completely and was willing to stake my life on it.

After a tense 15-minute wait Craig shouted: 'Go! Go!' I took a deep breath and whacked the motors wide open. The boat responded and we raced for the harbour entrance; now there would be no turning back once we had cleared it. We shot through the narrow gap in the rocks, and as we were about to clear it I heard myself blurt out: 'Oh, my God, we're in big shit, we're going to come unstuck in a big way out here today!'

The sight that confronted us was enough to give even King Neptune himself a panic attack. A wall of white, foaming water that looked to be four metres high was rushing in, broadside to us, not more than 200 metres away. I knew it would be virtually impossible to turn in the narrow rocky channel and rush back into the shelter of the harbour, so I shouted to the Frenchmen to hang on for all they were worth and aimed the bow at the sea end of the channel. If I could get out of the channel and swing the boat around to meet the wave head-on, we might survive; if I didn't, the wave would swamp us and fling us, boat and all, against the rocks.

The problem was that as far as I could tell the wave was going to win the race for the entrance by about 30 metres; if I was going to do anything about trying to get us out of this mess, it would have to be within about five seconds at most. I braced myself, focusing so hard on the foot of the wave that I literally forgot to breathe.

When the massive wave was less than 30 metres away I spun the helm hard to starboard, so that the boat swung violently around till it was head-on at the outcrop of rock at the end of the channel. The Frenchmen must have thought I had absolutely lost my mind to do something so suicidal. But there was method to my apparent madness, which was actually a calculated risk, albeit an extremely dangerous one.

We were less than ten metres from smashing head-on into the rock when the foot of the wave engulfed the protruding reef. The bow lifted sharply and missed the temporarily submerged rock by a few inches, after which the boat climbed up the almost vertical face of the wave at one hell of a pace.

About halfway up the wave the bow smashed through the more than vertical back wall of it. One moment we were about to be sucked under, the next we were flying through the air at least four metres clear of the water and then crashing down to the surface at such an acute angle that God alone knows how we avoided flipping over backwards.

In spite of all the noise and distractions, I heard a unanimous sigh of relief from the Frenchmen (and possibly from myself). My wild gamble had paid off! But there was nothing to cheer about, because the next batch of trouble was already rushing down on us as I struggled to bring the bucking and slewing boat under control again. I made use of my new-found knowledge and went straight at this wave at half-speed, throttling right back the moment that the bow started pushing through.

The mountain of water crashed down as the boat smashed through the wave, nearly washing all of us and our equipment overboard; to our relief the boat made a fairly soft landing this time, thanks to my throttling back at the right moment. In the very brief respite that followed I spent a few moments assessing our situation. Conclusion Number 1: We were in serious danger. Conclusion Number 2: There was no way we could turn back and run for the harbour without disastrous results. Conclusion Number 3: The first thing we needed to do – the only thing we could do, in fact – was to get behind the back line of the waves, which was still more than a kilometre away.

Gritting my teeth and alternately cursing myself and the Frenchmen, I devoted my full attention to getting to the back line. Somehow I managed to pull it off, and after a few more heart-stopping close shaves I finally bashed through the last wall of water. I did a little more thinking and decided to run the gauntlet to Dyer Island, in the hope that we would be able to find some shelter in its lee for a few hours till the sea (I hoped) had calmed down a bit, so that we would have a fighting chance of getting back to Kleinbaai.

But as we closed in on the island the sight that greeted us was even more frightening than what we had just gone through. The sea around the island was so wild that it made the onslaught on Kleinbaai look insignificant. On both sides of the island the giant swells were turning into massive waves that crashed onto the shallow reefs and exploded into towers of white, foaming water. The area in front of the island, where I had hoped to shelter, had eight-metre waves rushing past it into the kelp beds on the eastern side. Dyer Island wasn't going to be of any help at all. If I had been wearing seaboots my heart would have sunk into them.

As I dodged the waves, desperately contemplating my next move, Xavier found his voice and shouted: 'This is dangerous, Theo, this is dangerous! We must turn back immediately!' He couldn't have chosen a worse moment to start playing crybaby, and now I really blew my top.

'You stupid dickhead, I know it's dangerous!' I shouted. 'You weren't willing to take my word for it, you had to force the goddamn issue, you stupid arsehole!' Xavier obviously wasn't used to being spoken to like this, and he tensed up, but before he could say another word I cut him off at the knees. 'I don't want to hear any more bullshit from you – just shut your mouth and pray that you set foot on land again.'

He and Rock got the message loud and clear, and there wasn't a squeak out of them on our nightmare return trip (Xavier had been right: there was nothing else to do but go back). How the hell I ever managed to make it back that day I don't know; either I am an even better seaman than I had thought, or it really is proof that the Almighty loves fools and madmen.

But there was one important benefit: after their extremely close shave the Frenchmen became an easy and cooperative group to work with, and six weeks later the shoot was successfully completed.

In 1993 and 1994 we were involved in another very interesting shoot with the BBC Wildlife Unit. The BBC was attempting the most ambitious white shark shoot since the famous *Blue*

Water, White Death, and they had contacted the WSRP to work with them on this mammoth project.

The project started with Chris McFarlane, a BBC producer, being sent out to see us in early 1993. It was not a cordial relationship at first, because he managed to rub us all up the wrong way, but this changed later during the shoot and we became quite attached to him. Next to arrive were Paul Atkins, director, and Greg Marshal, the guy in charge of a new type of camera called the 'critter cam', the first-ever underwater camera specifically designed to be attached to a white shark. The critter cam's purpose was to record the shark's movements and behaviour when it was below the surface and invisible from the boat.

I sent Craig and one of his crew down to Gansbaai and Struisbaai to work with the BBC boys for a month, testing their equipment, scouting the area and checking to see if the critter cam would work the way it was supposed to. I was very proud when I heard that Craig had successfully become the first person in the world to attach a camera onto a free-swimming white shark. We always seemed to be doing something new and pioneering.

The BBC guys went away and were scheduled to return at the end of October with the full crew, so we had our work cut out with the preparation work: hiring houses, bringing in extra boats, organising extra crew ... and, of all things, building a camera tower in the middle of White Shark Alley.

Now, we were sailors and shark researchers, not a construction team, but being the anything-goes bunch that we were, we just said 'no problem' and got to constructing the tower in the middle of one of the meanest pieces of ocean in the world.

To be blunt, the channel was just about the worst place of all in which to undertake a do-it-yourself project of this magnitude. The water is six to seven metres deep and the spring tides push up another metre, the bottom of the channel is rocky, there is a strong surge through the channel, tons of kelp drifting around, and in rough weather the waves rush through like express trains.

On top of that the tower had to be sturdy enough to withstand this incredibly hostile environment for up to four months, safe for two cameramen to work from with expensive equipment and very stable, because the cameramen would be using powerful lenses and if it wasn't, the tight shots would be shaky. Not much to ask for.

We burnt the midnight oil and decided the tower would have to be about eight metres high in order to work in all the conditions the channel could, and doubtless would, throw at it. Our biggest headache was where to construct the damned thing. Should we build it on site in the water at the channel, or construct it on land and then tow it out to Dyer Island? We chewed this over at length and decided on the second option.

Now we had to find out if there was any place in the channel where the bottom was flat enough for the tower to stand straight up. Craig, Chris and Rob went over and, exhibiting their usual balls of steel, jumped into the water with four white sharks cruising around them and found just the spot.

We built the tower in sections that could be bolted together on the dock before being shipped to the island, and designed a combination of winches, cables and huge anchors in order to secure it. The idea was that once the tower had been positioned in place, divers would swim the four anchors out and physically wedge them in place behind bottom-rocks. Then the cables would be winched in till they were taut, holding the tower secure and solid.

One of our volunteers, Mike Hughes, belonged to a dive club and arranged for boats and a bunch of very eager and willing divers to assist us. We all met at Kleinbaai early one perfect morning to work out a game plan, then went to work. They were a great bunch, and in no time we had the tower bolted together and lying on its side. We then secured a bunch of big oil barrels to it, and used a truck and boat to push and pull the tower into the harbour.

Because of the fine weather and sea conditions it took us only about an hour to tow the tower out to the island and into the channel. When we arrived on site, the divers went into the water while two boats patrolled around as shark lookouts. One of the volunteers climbed onto the floating tower with a firearm and systematically shot the barrels at the base full of holes. The tower slowly sank into position as the barrels filled with water, just as we had planned it.

We cut the barrels loose and pulled them out while the divers guided the anchors into position and secured them, and Craig got the winches. Before long the WSRP's first excursion into marine architecture was complete and the tower was standing as solid as one of the surrounding rocks. By noon we were back at Kleinbaai, and naturally we had a big party to celebrate this rare triumph of humankind over nature.

The BBC's ten-man crew eventually arrived and we got to work with our four boats and ten crew members – quite a sweat to maintain and sustain. We spent the next three months at Dyer Island and Struisbaai, an exhausting and not uneventful time. We often worked in extreme conditions, and at various times we lost the critter cam and were forced to carry out dangerous night-time searches for it, one of the boats was destroyed and we almost lost our big 45-footer in a storm. But we ended up with some of the most spectacular white shark footage ever taken, so fine that today, a decade later, this documentary is still the benchmark for all the others.

And the tower? Well, it did its job perfectly and it was so sturdy, in fact, that it remained standing for another four months after the shoot before being flattened by a particularly violent storm. The police then came out and dragged it into deeper water because it was a navigational hazard in the channel. So, unfortunately, nothing remains of The Tower That Theo and His Boys Built. But it wasn't bad for a first effort.

TEN

Golden days ... and stormy ones

Some golden years followed as the WSRP's reputation and expertise as the leading collector of scientific data on white sharks rapidly became recognised and respected around the world. We enjoyed a high national and international profile, with biologists and wildlife film-makers from many other countries coming to visit and work with us; we were involved in no fewer than 23 international documentary film shoots.

I found myself in a situation I had never contemplated, even in my wildest dreams. Here I was, a rough-and-ready reborn shark hunter without one iota of formal academic learning to my name, at the helm of a very small, much underfunded group which was definitely out of its depth at times but was fast becoming one of the world's most progressive shark research and conservation organisations.

Call it the fervour of the newly converted, but I had become a very dedicated champion of the great white shark and all its broader family and was almost obsessed with my drive to save these animals from the destruction of humankind. I was so focused that I only saw my objectives, and paid little attention to such things as diplomacy and playing politics. In my naivety I believed that everyone else could see the objectives as clearly as I thought I could, and that obviously they would be right behind me.

Little did I know that the arena in which I was battling for the salvation of the white shark was full of huge egos and cut-throat politics. No names, no pack drill, as they used to say in the army, but there were quite a few people who were terribly envious of the high profile we were receiving, in spite of our blatant lack of degrees, funding and official recognition. The result was that powerful forces came into play – and they were not working for the good of the WSRP.

I first became aware of this when a ghost from the past appeared in the shape of a man called Trail Wittuhn. Wittuhn claimed to be collecting scientific data on white sharks on behalf of the Oceanographic Research Institute (ORI) in Durban by hooking and then tagging them. Wittuhn's method was to take out clients who would hook white sharks and fight them to a standstill, after which he would tag them and cut them loose.

I was furious about this. The white shark was now at the top of the protected species list, along with whales and dolphins, and hooking them flew in the face of the measures that were supposed to protect them.

There were three very good reasons for the lure-and-tag method the WSRP had used so successfully. Firstly, hooking white sharks was a needlessly cruel practice that resulted in hours of desperate struggle. Secondly, sharks have large blood vessels in the head and gill area, and the hours-long pressure of the hook's steel trace was likely to cause massive damage and bleeding. Thirdly, the overall stress and trauma would certainly result in a high mortality rate. Yet Wittuhn was being allowed to go ahead and do his own thing.

In fairness to Wittuhn, he didn't try to disguise himself as a quasi-scientist or conservationist, but stated publicly for all who cared to listen that he was a commercial fisherman who caught and tagged white sharks because the ORI paid him to do so.

But there was more to it than that, as I discovered when I offered to teach him the passive tagging procedure WSRP was using. Wittuhn was not interested. Overseas big-game fishermen paid him to take them out to hook and fight the sharks before they were tagged and released, and he was not willing to give up this source of income as a favour to conservation.

I just couldn't believe that South Africa's historic move to protect the white shark was being laughed at by Wittuhn and his employers, so I declared war by going to the authorities, armed with some well-reasoned arguments, to demand that they stop this character's activities, which were surely a contravention of the law.

Surely? Boy, was I wildly mistaken! I went in with no idea of the heavy-duty politics and internal agendas at work, and I got exactly nowhere. Wittuhn was hooked up to the ORI, the ORI had been running a hook-and-tag programme for decades and they were not about to stop simply because I was blowing my top.

My one-man war wasn't aimed primarily at Wittuhn. He was only an ignorant small-town commercial fisherman, just as I had been in my shark-hunting days, and he made his living from the sea. From his point of view there was nothing wrong with exploiting the situation for profit – the scientists were paying him to tag white sharks, so he was tagging white sharks and providing his clients with some sport in the process; the research derived from the tagging was none of his business.

I didn't allow myself to be discouraged by the initial setbacks, and I made so much noise that eventually the powers-that-were couldn't simply ignore me any longer. But their response wasn't a positive one: the Department of Sea Fisheries merely issued the ORI and Wittuhn with a special permit to hook and tag great white sharks.

This *really* made me hit the roof. Here we were, bragging that we were the first country to protect white sharks, but we allowed them to be hooked in the same cruel and destructive fashion that had been used in the bad old anything-goes days. The only essential difference between the old days and the Wittuhn modification was that a shark was released once it had been caught. But by then, as I've said, much of the damage had been done.

In characteristic fashion, I carried on raising as much of a row as I could, and after a while the noise and pressure started to take its toll on both Wittuhn and the ORI. In what looked to me like an attempt at self-justification, Wittuhn and the ORI approached a film company and persuaded the producer to do a documentary on his hooking-and-tagging methodology.

The film crew spent about a week going out with Wittuhn and one of his clients, and then the producer contacted me to tell me that he had been very disturbed by what he had witnessed and encountered.

According to the producer, the first two white sharks to be hooked by Wittuhn's client had been lost when the terminal traces parted, leaving each of them to swim away, trailing about eight metres of cable and a plastic buoy still attached to the embedded hook. He added that when a white shark was finally brought up to the boat it was in such a state of exhaustion that it was bleeding profusely from its mouth, gills and anus.

He was not a scientist, the producer said, or an authority on hunting big-game sharks, but in his opinion this shark was very close to death, if not actually dead already, by the time Wittuhn had tagged and released it.

He would show me the footage, he said, and asked if he and his team could spend two days observing the WSRP's luring-and-tagging method so that a comparison could be drawn. We were only too happy, and in due course the film team went to sea with us. After we had tagged our second shark on the first day at sea the producer said that in his opinion the hooking-and-tagging method was totally unacceptable.

Six weeks later, when the documentary was screened on TV and the contrast between the two methods was graphically illustrated, it became clear that the viewing public agreed with him. Lacking the facts, the general public's perception had been that there wasn't much wrong with the hook-and-release method. But when the public was made aware of the true facts of the matter there was a dramatic change of attitude, followed by a loud and sustained outcry.

To my surprise, even this had no immediate effect because instead of seizing the initiative and taking action, the Department of Sea Fisheries reacted like a typical bureaucracy and simply went deaf, dumb and blind on the entire subject. I bearded the acting Director of Sea Fisheries in his den, only to be informed that his department did not consider the great white shark to be an exploitable resource, and as a result it was not high on the Sea Fisheries priority list. My response to this official evasion of responsibility is better left to the reader's imagination.

I didn't stop, however, and eventually I wore the Department of Sea Fisheries down to the point where it revoked Wittuhn's permit to hook white sharks. But this didn't stop Wittuhn from taking clients out. He denied adamantly that he was doing anything wrong. He was now fishing for other shark species, he said, and he couldn't help it if great white sharks took his bait. I didn't accept this argument, and, needless to say, some very bad blood developed between us.

I didn't care, and I am sure Wittuhn didn't either. I hated what he had done and was doing, but I couldn't help thinking that in my ignorant shark-hunting days I would probably have taken the same attitude. In a way I actually respected the man a little for the extremely hard stand he took to protect what he believed he was entitled to. I had been fortunate enough to realise the terrible damage I had been doing, and he hadn't.

It was my first brush with the sharks on the landward side of the surf, but certainly not the last. I got bitten by them sometimes and bled a little, but there were also good times that helped to heal the tooth-marks. And, of course, there was that wonderful team that made up the White Shark Research Project – the real heroes of the world of white shark conservation.

What made the whole thing even more remarkable was that virtually the entire team comprised volunteers who gave unstintingly of their time and skills without being paid a red cent, because the WSRP did not generate enough funds even to cover their day-to-day expenses.

The first volunteers were, of course, my Norma – who contributed both morally and financially to the project – my son Craig and my daughters Tracy and Cherie. Another early volunteer, and a very welcome one, too, was Len Compagno, then one of the world's most acclaimed great white shark researchers, who joined as the WSRP's resident volunteer scientist because, as a permanent employee of the South African Museum, he couldn't be involved full time (and we didn't have the financial resources to pay him, anyway).

And then, of course, there were the volunteer boat crews whose names pop up throughout this book. One of them, Liam Reynolds, was to die at a tragically young age, but not before he had made a great personal contribution to the project and become a respected friend.

It was through their dedication and sheer hard work that the WSRP became the world leader in white shark tagging, population dynamic studies and behavioural data collection within two years of its founding, in spite of the serious dearth of infrastructure and resources.

Finding operating funds was always a struggle because the WSRP was solely dependent on its own scanty resources, and we did all sorts of things to raise some cash. One that worked very well – although not entirely without some hitches – was an educational cycle tour sponsored by Nampak, the well-known packaging company.

The idea was that businessmen working for or doing business with Nampak would promote the image of the white shark and the WSRP by cycling all the way from Pretoria, a distance of 1 700 kilometres, which would take ten days to cover. They would arrive in Cape Town on 13 March 1991. They would be accompanied by some of us from the WSRP (cycling or riding in two minibuses supplied by Mazda).

En route the cyclists would visit the schools that had joined in the fundraising drive, and at each we would do an educational presentation on the sharks. Each school would also do a project on the subject, with a prize for the best one.

Many of the projects were of a very high standard, but the one that stood out above all the rest was produced by Cambridge High School in the east-coast city of East London, which was ultimately declared the winner of the Nampak Cycle Tour White Shark Competition.

When the leg-weary cyclists were 30 kilometres from East London, those of us who were not cycling with them drove on ahead in one minibus to help the school to prepare for their arrival. We need not have worried. Cambridge High was ready for them, and they were led up to its premises by the school's band and drum majorettes, while parents, teachers and pupils lined the route. We could see how the tired cyclists perked up at this royal welcome.

The assembly hall had been given over to a display of such high standard that it compared favourably with some of the top ones I had seen at the recent South African Wildlife Expo, and the school choir sang a beautiful song called 'The King of the Deep', which they had composed themselves in honour of the white shark.

Those kids sang it with such passion that I couldn't hold back my tears. Naturally I was embarrassed by this outburst of emotion, like any good old macho South African male, but then I glanced around at rest of our group who were also sitting on the stage ... and they were wiping their eyes as well.

After this wonderful reception, the cyclists left East London in high spirits the next morning, carried on down that favourite tourist destination, the Garden Route, and on 12 March finally arrived at Hottentots Holland High School in Strand, about 55 kilometres from the endpoint at the South African Museum in Cape Town.

This school, too, had gone to a lot of trouble with its white shark display project and gave the cyclists an enthusiastic welcome. The next morning they set off on the final leg to Cape Town, with stopoffs scheduled at De Grendel High School and Rondebosch Boys' High School which had won the first prize of R15 000 in the previous year's fundraiser.

Things started to unravel a little when we and the cyclists arrived at De Grendel at nine o'clock, dead on schedule, only to find that, as a very embarrassed headmaster told me, the school had entirely forgotten about the arrival of the cycle tour! I was bitterly disappointed to hear this, and at least as embarrassed as the headmaster himself, and it was a rather unhappy group of cyclists who got going on the last 12 kilometres to the endpoint at the South African Museum.

The fiasco at De Grendel resulted in their arriving an hour early at the museum. There we encountered a second faux pas when I found nothing had been done to welcome the cyclists. What it amounted to was that these men had sacrificed their time and effort to cycle almost 2 000 kilometres in support of the WSRP, and there wasn't even a cup of tea awaiting them on arrival. The cyclists – not to mention the WSRP members – were so disheartened that I could see the enthusiasm the trip had generated just draining away.

Well, to hell with that! I called my small band of shark-brothers together and we decided to run with the ball. We went over the planning for the end-of-trip function, which was to be held in the museum's Whale Well two days later and threw everything we had into making it a really memorable occasion, which included bringing in extra wine, food and champagne.

Our efforts paid off, and the function was a roaring success. More than 100 school representatives, sponsors, dignitaries and media people attended, and the festive atmosphere wiped out the bad taste left by the earlier disappointments.

Len gave a good slide presentation on where and how we could spend the income on research, and then Dr Cluver, the museum director, came up with a speech praising Len and the museum for all the WSRP's achievements. I wasn't happy about this, to say the least, because the clear impression was that I had had little to do with any of the WSRP's achievements. This was not only inaccurate – everybody likes his contributions to be recognised, after all – but also weakened my position in future dealings with potential sponsors. But for once I kept my cool, apart from some teeth-grinding.

Gerhard Visser of Mazda levelled the playing fields, though, when he got up to praise me for my work. He gave me full credit for all the successes of the Mazda foundation's involvement with the WSRP. I was, of course, relieved and proud, but I could sense that the WSRP's relationship with the museum was in the process of changing.

A couple of days later I had an intensive discussion with Len, after which I had an idea of what was happening. I was suffering the fate of explorers throughout history. I had gone where (as they used to say in *Star Trek*) no man had gone before, hacking out the pathway into the unknown. Now, with the pathway open, the organisation men were beginning to stream in and the rugged trailblazer's task was more or less done.

Well, this old trailblazer wasn't quite ready to hang up his hat just yet, and it was clear that a parting of ways was looming. I began looking for alternative headquarters. I started negotiating with the developers of the Two Oceans Aquarium and they gave the WSRP temporary headquarters at the V&A Waterfront where we could set up the very first white shark display and education centre in southern Africa. The old building we were allocated needed considerable cleaning up, but it had the necessary potential and we got to work.

We begged and borrowed whatever we could lay hands on from wherever it was available, and cemented everything together with many litres of elbow-grease. The result was a really good display that attracted more than 30 000 visitors in the next two years, ranging from schoolchildren to members of the local public and tourists. And apart from the sheer satisfaction of the thing, it also provided the WSRP with a modest but steady stream of income.

The creation of the shark education centre didn't mean the end of the WSRP's relationship with the South African Museum, and we went on cooperating via Len Compagno till 1994. Then, just after we had completed the huge BBC film shoot, Len acquired a new staff member named Mark Marks.

As we understood it, Marks was going to team up with Craig on the WSRP's field research, but it seemed that his own understanding differed from ours. This became clear in our very first conversation, when Marks told me that he was going to be taking over all field operations and I was expected to return all the field research equipment to the museum, including the boat.

This came completely out of the blue, so that I thought he was joking at first. Then I realised that he was dead serious. I told him to take a hike and telephoned Len to tell him that there was no way I was going to upset Craig's applecart – he had developed a fantastic team which just got on with the job with no complaints from anybody. Marks would have to find his place way down on the bottom rungs of the ladder or he was not welcome to work with the WSRP field unit.

This didn't have any effect, and as time went by I realised that Len had no real control over Marks. From this time an estrangement began to arise between us. I wasn't quite sure about the reasons for it, but it was definitely there, and I felt sad about it, because the two of us had done so much in such a short time; we had made history, in fact, which is something not everyone can say when they look back on their lives.

The deathblow to our friendship came in early 1995 over a dispute about co-authoring an article on the scientific data on white shark population dynamics that the WSRP had collected over the past five years. The upshot of it was that Craig and I were invited to submit a paper to a leading scientific journal. It was a tall order, seeing that we had less than three months to summarise five years of work, but we got it in on time. I couldn't conceal my pride when the paper in question received favourable reviews and eventual publication.

It was the end of our friendship, however, and we parted in a cloud of mutual recriminations. Today, many years later and with the benefit of hindsight, I realise that actually the fault lay in the fact that we were both blinkered by absolute tunnel vision as we pursued our quest, two totally different people who were both fixated on the same ultimate destination but travelled towards it by different routes instead of finding a way to combine our energies.

The fact remains that the two of us were right in the forefront of the movement to make the great white shark a protected species, and that achievement is something that will survive any differences we had along the way, no matter what ill feeling they might have caused at the time.

ELEVEN

Fish out of water in the new white shark arena

Nowadays people tend to forget how politically isolated South Africa was in the 1980s and early 1990s. On the nonpolitical lower level at which I operated, this resulted in a rather informal way of doing business. If we needed to stay over on Dyer Island, for example, or needed whale or seal meat for bait, or wanted to work in sensitive areas, a telephone call or two was usually enough to get us what we wanted.

Nobody was particularly interested in the great white shark from a scientific point of view, so the fact that we were spending large sums of private funding on researching these animals was good news for the authorities, because we were gathering potentially valuable information at no cost to them.

But in 1994, the year of the new democracy, South Africa opened up to the world again for the first time in many years, and suddenly it wasn't politically incorrect to visit our shores any more. By the end of that year the first outside researchers started appearing, shark tourism was emerging as a mini industry in its own right and film crews were becoming a positive hindrance to our research work.

By the end of 1995 everything was changing so quickly that I couldn't keep up. The white shark was fast becoming a valuable 'exploitable commodity', to use a favourite Sea Fisheries phrase, for both scientists and commercial operators. And as more and more value was added – whether it involved money or prestige – the purity of the past five years began to fade.

It wasn't a totally one-sided process. A few purists like Craig and I tried to keep things unsullied, but it was like trying to stamp out a huge veld fire with our feet. Craig, who was always more diplomatic than I was, realised that if you couldn't beat them the best thing was to join them and try to limit the damage from within the system, but that wasn't my style, and eventually I decided to call it a day.

I resigned from the WSRP and handed over to Craig. It was a very difficult decision and it took me a long time to come to terms with it, but I knew it was the right move. The white shark saga had become a terribly ugly and controversial industry, with constant fighting between various large egos. I had become embroiled in many fights and controversies, but all for the wrong reasons. So it was the right time to pull the plug.

I settled back into normal life, developing my own company and taking many holidays, and as time went by, I got great white sharks out of my system. Or so I thought. Craig continued to run the WSRP for another two and a half years and I sat back and observed all the problems he was forced to deal with. There was so much fighting and controversy in the white shark arena that most of his time was taken up just wading through all the bullshit.

Finally I advised him to dissolve the WSRP and start his own company. He was a married man now who had to look to his future, and there was no money in white shark research, although it was a full-time occupation. Craig felt that way, too. In 1997 he wound the WSRP down, and with his wife, Jytte, founded a commercial diving, filming and research company called White Shark Projects. The company went on to become a leader in its field, which did not surprise me at all. Craig was an exceptional person and, if I say so myself, had had a good teacher.

While all this was happening, my renewed connection with white sharks was drifting nearer, although I didn't quite realise it yet. They and I were still to have a long involvement, and at times not a pleasant one, which among other things led to my arrest, the impounding of my boat and a long, protracted journey through the law courts.

I don't know how much attention I would have paid even if I had realised what lay in the future, because I had far more serious preoccupations. Norma finally lost her very brave battle against cancer, and my life decayed into a dark and gloomy place with no light or joy in it. I was so full of pain and grief that all I really wanted to do was blow my brains out.

The only thing that held me back from killing myself was a promise I had made to Norma only weeks before she died. Every time I was about to give in to my grief and despair she would put her own suffering aside and tell me: 'My love, when I'm gone you'll have to be there for our children and their little ones. Promise me you'll look after them.' And of course I promised, without any conditions or provisions.

A couple of years passed and gradually, as the worst pain of Norma's passing faded, I began to glue my shattered life back together. I still needed a lodestone to guide my journey through the rest of my life, and the man who gave it to me was Solomon Vanqua, my longtime employee and good friend.

Why not work with white sharks again, he suggested. And there it was, the lodestone I had been seeking. I wasted no time in submitting a well-motivated application for a white shark dive permit to Marine and Coastal Management (MCM). After three weeks without a response I telephoned MCM to ask about the fate of my application and was told that there had been a delay in the process, so that it would be another week or two before any permits would be issued. Firmly under the impression that I would be successful in my efforts, I decided to be patient and wait for it.

Soon after this conversation Craig telephoned me and said that all white shark permits had expired, so that the entire dive industry was working without them. There was no reason why I should not start operating right away, he said, since MCM had failed to issue the permits by the due date. This made sense to me, and within days I was operational.

My first day as a white shark dive operator started well. My stepson, Donovan van der Watt, and I put to sea that morning from Simon's Town with five clients on board and headed for Seal Island. We arrived at about nine o'clock, dropped anchor and soon had a well-established chum slick spreading. By noon, however, no shark had made an appearance yet, and I was beginning to become concerned.

I told Donovan to step up the chumming tempo, put two fresh tuna heads on the bait lines and started willing the sharks to show up. By half past three, however, they were still staying away and I had the embarrassing task of explaining to the clients that although we had tried our very best, there just couldn't be any guarantees when working with wild creatures.

That turned out to be truer than I thought. Donovan had pulled in one of the baits and was busy uncleating the second rope when I spotted a large, unmistakable shape slowly rising to the surface about 20 metres downstream. My pulse started to race with all the old excitement. 'Yes, you beauty!' I bellowed. 'Come to papa!'

The clients and Donovan whipped around and stared at me in amazement, then joined me in joyful chorus as I whooped with joy and pointed to the new arrival. The shark, a female about four metres long and probably weighing about 1 000 kilos, surfaced into clear view, and she was one hell of a sight to behold. *Yeah, man,* I thought, *this is living again!*

The beautifully proportioned killing machine made herself right at home, zeroing in on the remaining bait and devouring it in one swift gulp. In record time we had both lines re-baited and back in the water, and the chum slick going again. The shark responded with a show that lasted an hour and a half and was so enthralling that the dive cage remained high and dry on the stern, and the wetsuits and scuba equipment lay unused in the stowage locker. I think we would have interacted with her till after dark if we hadn't run out of both bait and chum.

Then we became involved in another display that was a good deal less enthralling. While Donovan and I cleaned the chum bucket and other equipment before stowing everything away in preparation for our return to Simon's Town, I noticed a fisheries patrol boat bearing down on us from about three kilometres away. We carried on with what we were doing and were just about ready to up-anchor when it drew up about 20 metres off our port side.

The inspector on the boat shouted to us to stop lifting the anchor, and for the next ten minutes, he filmed and photographed Albatross from stem to stern. When his official photo shoot was over, he and a fellow-inspector launched a rubber dinghy and came on board, taking Donovan and me up to the flying bridge while his assistant questioned the clients. In the meantime the shark had got bored and moved off.

The inspector asked if I had a white shark dive permit. I replied that I was awaiting the issue of a permit, and that currently there were no valid permits in the entire white shark industry because his employers at MCM had allowed them to expire.

I don't think this answer pleased him, because he and his colleague proceeded to search the boat and photograph the chum bucket and dive cage, informing me in passing that I was in deep trouble and I must follow them back to port. I wasn't willing even to consider this and flatly refused.

The inspector persisted, at which my hackles began to rise, and soon a heated exchange was in progress between us. My point, which I made very emphatically, was that in my opinion I had done nothing wrong or illegal and therefore saw no reason to obey his demand. This went on for a bit and then, when it became obvious that he was losing control of the situation, he backed off and instructed me to report to the Simon's Town police station at ten o'clock the following morning.

When I rolled up the next morning a policeman took my fingerprints and informed me that I was being formally charged with 'disturbing a white shark without a permit'. I couldn't believe my ears and asked the cop to repeat what he had said. He did, and I couldn't help bursting out laughing.

'It's absolutely ridiculous that you actually need a permit to disturb a white shark,' I said when I had sobered up again. 'I'm sorry, but this charge against me is an absolute joke.' The policeman either lacked a sense of humour or chose to ignore what I had said. I was to be in court the next morning, he said.

When I appeared before the magistrate the following morning I pleaded not guilty and asked that the case be thrown out. The magistrate declined, and the prosecutor asked for a bond of R500 000 to be placed on my boat. I nearly wet my pants, and for the first time started taking the matter very seriously.

I managed to plead the bond down to R50 000, got out of there and started looking for a hotshot attorney. One recommended to me suggested I plead guilty and throw myself at the court's mercy, so I fired him before even hiring him and decided to defend myself at my trial, to which I was looking forward with keen anticipation.

I had plenty of time to prepare and refine my defence, because during the next seven months the case was postponed five times. After the fifth postponement I telephoned the prosecutor and complained about the delay. She replied that she was willing to fine me a mere R1 500 if I pleaded guilty. I turned her down on the spot. I was not willing to plead guilty, I said, and in fact I wished to face my accusers in court.

This intervention obviously had a good effect, because a week later the trial finally got underway. The first prosecution witness was the fisheries inspector who had originally laid the charge. He stated that when he had approached our boat off Seal Island, he had observed that we had a shark cage on board. When he and his colleague boarded the boat he had seen a chum bucket on the deck, and both the clients and I had confirmed that we had observed and interacted with a white shark. He had concluded that there was sufficient evidence of a crime, and so he had laid a charge against me.

Cross-examining him, I asked how large the shark that I had allegedly disturbed had been. He replied that he had not seen the shark, and when I pressed him some more he admitted that he had never seen a white shark in his life. Then I asked him to describe to the court how I had disturbed the shark 'which you incidentally never laid an eye on'. This reduced him to silence.

When the magistrate ran out of patience and ordered him to answer the question, the inspector blurted out that we had had a chum bucket and shark cage on board, and therefore we must have been disturbing white sharks. This reasoning elicited chuckles from everyone present in the courtroom except, of course, the hapless inspector.

But I wasn't done with him yet. Had he observed any chum or baiting material on board the boat? He replied that he had not. And had he seen any of us in physical contact with a white shark at any time? The answer was 'no' again.

The second fisheries inspector then gave evidence, and when I climbed into him during cross-examination he contradicted his colleague's evidence to such an extent that the magistrate said: 'Mr Ferreira, do you remember when you requested that I chuck this case out of court on your first appearance before me?'

I said I did, and he responded: 'Well, you can ask me that same question again.' When I did, he promptly dismissed the case and chastised both the state and MCM for wasting the court's and my time.

I walked out feeling pretty good, and it dawned on me that I had made history again as the first person ever to be criminally charged with a white shark-related offence.

With the court case now behind me, I submitted another highly motivated application for a dive permit to MCM. This led to a seven-month-long hiatus in which my repeated attempts to find out what was happening were fobbed off with a variety of unsatisfactory excuses. Eventually I became so fed up with this farcical and frustrating business that I contacted the Public Protector's office.

A meeting was duly arranged at their offices, where I handed them copies of all my correspondence with MCM. The advocate handling my complaint agreed that I had been poorly treated and said she would go into the matter, promising to keep me informed of any developments.

About two weeks after my meeting with the Public Protector, a Mr Buthelezi at MCM made contact with me. He appeared to be genuinely concerned and interested, and assured me that a Mr Marius Diemont, a legal advisor to MCM, would be contacting me to address my problem.

About nine o'clock the next evening, my phone rang. It was Marius Diemont on the line. I was so surprised at this flood of attention after the months of battling to get even a slight response from MCM that it took me about 30 seconds to get a coherent conversation going. Was my luck changing at last?

We spent about three minutes discussing the background to my problems and then he suggested I come to the MCM offices to thrash the matter out. Two days later I went to see him, and we debated for about an hour about the merits of my application and MCM's response. Eventually he conceded that I had been poorly treated, promising that he would investigate further and get back to me in due course.

He was true to his word and came back to me within a few days. Not only that, but with some positive advice that was so unexpected after almost a year of frustration that it was one of the rare occasions in my life when I had very little to say.

He had made headway with MCM's senior management, he said. To make progress, he added, 'You're going to have to wipe the slate clean, bury the hatchet and start afresh with them.'

Having said that, he added that the chances of my application being approved would depend on the way I approached the MCM management, and he would fax me an outline of the important points I would need to address in my motivation. There was no reason why my application should not succeed if I followed the outline he suggested.

This turn of events was so unexpected and exciting that I found myself whooping with uncontrolled joy as soon as I had put down the phone. Soon afterwards the fax he had promised arrived. I didn't waste a moment – I settled right down at my computer and spent many hours preparing and revising the all-important document. I didn't stop till the early hours of the next morning, when I had finally satisfied myself that I couldn't make the motivation any better than it already was. I printed it in preparation for faxing it off to the MCM before flopping into bed for a few hours' sleep.

About a week later a very upbeat and friendly Marius Diemont phoned me, and even before he broached the subject of the call I knew from his manner that he had succeeded in fulfilling the promise he had made to me. Then he said the magic words: 'Theo, your application has been approved,' adding 'There's one important point I want you to keep in mind. I've gone out of my way to help you with this one, so please don't let me down.'

It's strange how one good act can change your entire state of mind. Within seconds I went from a toxic pile of accumulated frustration and anger to something like grovelling gratitude, willing to cooperate in any way necessary. Then I asked the crucial question: 'Tell me when I can start operating?' To which he replied: 'Your exemption has been approved, and you can start tomorrow, if you wish,' adding that a confirmatory letter would be mailed to me.

I threw a celebratory dinner with my family and loyal staff, after which we got down to work. Within a week we had kick-started the business, and six days later we set out for Seal Island with our first five clients on board.

We were full of high spirits and expectation as we neared Seal Island about 30 minutes after leaving Simon's Town, and none more so than myself. I had been denied my much-needed white shark 'fix' for too long, and I could feel my pulse quickening in anticipation of the thrill I would feel at coming face to face with these mighty predators again.

There was a lot of chatter and excitement as we got the chum slick going and then dropped our lines, baited with tuna heads. It was a perfect day with good visibility, and the chances of attracting some real whoppers were excellent. Unfortunately nobody told the sharks that, and as the hours passed the bubbling excitement and cheerful banter started drying up and turning into bored silence, broken only by someone asking for another Coke or something to nibble on.

I conceded defeat when the sun had swung past high noon position and begun heading slowly towards the west and bedtime. I called Donovan to one side and told him to chum for another 15 minutes; if no shark appeared we would call it a day. The minutes passed one by one without any result, and with a heavy heart I said: 'OK, guys, let's close up shop and start heading home.' Glumly Donovan started hauling in the bait line, and then quite suddenly he screamed out: 'There's a shark behind the boat!'

I thought he was indulging in some pretty ill-timed humour and turned to tear him off a strip. But a large dorsal and tail fin broke the water less than three metres from the stern, and my rebuke turned into a wild cry of joy (and some excited profanities, to be honest) as a magnificent white shark of about four metres cruised into view.

When I eventually got my right mind back I realised that everybody else was just as excited as I was. And from then on everything was 100 per cent. The great white shark rose valiantly to the occasion and put on a bravura show for the clients till the shadows really started lengthening and we finally had to tear ourselves away from the amazing sea creature that had given us such a magical gift.

The clients weren't any happier than I was. I understood now how much I had missed interacting with the great whites that had occupied so much of my thoughts for so many years. *Thank you, thank you, Marius Diemont*, I thought as we headed back to Simon's Town. I was back where I belonged.

Our letter from the MCM arrived in the post about three weeks after Marius Diemont's call, and I decided that I had been forced to fight so hard and obdurately for this piece of paper that I was going to have it laminated as a reminder of how bitter and sweet my battle to obtain it had been.

No one could imagine the hurt, humiliation, anger and frustration I had suffered to obtain it, and I swore that there was no way I would expose myself to such trauma ever again. So much for foresight. I would be in trouble again, and not too far into the future either.

It soon became evident that our boat, *Albatross*, although very comfortable and luxurious, was a rather slow and cumbersome beast for trips to the island and back, and in addition was a bitch in strong winds when coming on and off the mooring. As we now had an exemption from prosecution and there appeared to be no reason why we would not be successful with our permit application, I didn't see any reason why I shouldn't sell *Albatross* and buy a more suitable boat.

I flew to Durban a week later and found the perfect boat, a ten-metre Gee-Cat with two 150-horsepower Yamaha outboards. Two weeks our new boat, which I had christened *Shark Aholic*, arrived at Cape Town on a cargo ship. She was unloaded the same night, fuelled up and moored at the Royal Cape Yacht Club.

The next morning at about half past six we – myself, Solomon Vanqua, Donovan and Eugene van der Watt – left Cape Town docks for *Shark Aholic's* shakedown cruise to Simon's Town. When we hit the open sea I gently opened the throttles, and the boat responded like a thoroughbred racehorse. Within minutes I was confident that I had one hell of a boat that would serve us faithfully in all conditions.

Given my talent for landing in the dwang, *Shark Aholic's* maiden voyage wasn't as uneventful as it might have been, and before we got to Simon's Town we became involved in a sideshow that was half drama and half comedy.

We made great time towards Cape Point and soon caught up with a large fleet of fishing boats off the Slangkop Lighthouse, which was heavily engaged in hauling out large numbers of snoek, that iconic Cape fighting and eating fish. All four of us were passionate anglers, and we soon had our lures sinking into the crystal-clear Atlantic Ocean.

Some exciting and profitable hook-and-line activity followed, because the hordes of snoek were so hungry that they were taking anything we threw at them, but were not giving up without a fight. Within 45 minutes we had landed about 16 of them, near the top end of our legal quota, so I called for 'lines up' and prepared to move off.

As I started the motors and got under way, I noticed a Marine and Coastal Management patrol boat slowly weaving its way through the fishing boats near us, but I didn't pay it any attention. Then, after about five minutes, I happened to look around and noticed that the patrol boat was following directly behind us, about a sea mile away.

I remember thinking that if they weren't so far behind I would almost be inclined to suspect that they were following us for some reason best known to themselves. But they fell so far behind as I increased speed that I dismissed the idea.

Then half an hour later a police patrol boat flagged us down, and the senior cop asked us why we were running away from the MCM boat. I was so astonished that I burst out laughing.

'What the hell are you talking about?' I said. 'I'm not running away from anybody.' He shouted back: 'They told us you were running from them, and that we should apprehend you.'

To cut a long story short, the police boat kept us company for the next 20 minutes while the MCM craft caught up with us. Then followed an unpleasant few minutes when the inspector, having carefully counted our catch to make sure we were within the limit, demanded to see our angling permits ... which, I now remembered, we had not brought with us.

After a long wrangle and the application of a strong dose of bullshit from my side to divert his attention, the inspector finally went on his way after making me promise to fax copies of the permits to him. This done, we went our respective ways, and I was certain that the past two years' bad odour between the MCM and myself would now fade away.

It took us about a week to sort our new boat out and have her surveyed and registered by the authorities. Since I had spent a substantial amount of money on the boat and the marketing side, it was a pleasant relief to hear our telephone start ringing with calls from prospective clients.

Over the next few months we had reasonable success, and slowly but surely our business took off. By mid-November of 2003 things were going well, the only damper being the strong southeasters, which often kept us off the water. But there were many good days, too, when we were able to run out to Seal Island and have a lot of joy and excitement with the white sharks we encountered there.

I remember one of these days particularly well. Soon after leaving Seal Island on our return trip, we encountered a school of dolphins and some whales about halfway between the island and Simon's Town. It was a magnificent and almost unreal experience to find ourselves suddenly surrounded by about 30 whales and what must have been at least 1 000 dolphins. It was such a magical moment that I switched off the outboards and we drifted through a living carpet of frolicking animals that stretched out at least two kilometres in all directions.

I was awestruck by the sheer beauty and friendliness of these wonderful creatures, and Donovan and Eugene were so taken by the sheer magic of the moment that they decided to go overboard and swim with the dolphins.

For the next 20 minutes the most amazing interaction took place between the boys and the dolphins, which zoomed right up to them in a marvelously open and friendly manner. It was the sort of experience that not only draws you closer to nature but actually makes life worth living.

So it was a good time. Our shark-diving operation was now running smoothly and steadily picking up business, and I was enjoying this new lease on life so much that I started mellowing toward MCM and was building a much more relaxed and open relationship with them, right to the point where I could make rapid contact with their senior staff. It was a refreshing change from the adversarial situation of a little earlier.

TWELVE

False Bay becomes an attack zone ...
and I finally swallow the anchor

An unprecedented number of incidents and attacks on humans involving white sharks took place in False Bay during and after the first 18 months or so of our activities as cage dive operators. For many years there had not been one fatal attack in the bay, and only an occasional non-fatal skirmish. Then in five years there were more attacks resulting in death or serious injury than there had been in the previous half-century.

A surfer was killed by a white shark while working the waves off Scarborough. Some months later a surfer from Muizenberg had his leg bitten off, suffering such serious injury that his survival was nothing short of a miracle. Within a year, an elderly woman was fatally injured during her daily swim. About ten months later a young lifesaver going to the aid of his brother, who had been confronted by a white shark, ended up becoming the victim instead and lost one leg below the knee.

In addition to these fatal and near-fatal attacks, surfers and paddle-skiers had many close encounters – ranging from minor to serious – and I lost count of how many times the beaches in the immediate area were cleared as a result of great white shark activity nearby.

This alarming new trend stirred up a lot of public anger against the shark-dive industry in the bay area. The most common accusation was that the practice of chumming to attract white sharks and then allowing them to feed on the baits was conditioning them to associate boats and people with food.

From my wide experience of white shark behaviour, however, I was convinced that this was not the case, so I did what I could to clarify some of the misconceptions and calm the hysterical reactions, while simultaneously trying to establish exactly what role the dive operators had played in the escalation of the number of attacks.

My reasoning was as follows: imagine a typical situation in which there is a surfer or bather near the backline of the waves, a large white shark cruising past a short distance further out to sea and a dive operator chumming the water in the direction of the swimmers, with the shark between him or her and the boat. Common logic, one would think, would positively scream out that this would almost certainly result in a shark attack.

But I concluded that according to shark rather than human logic the exact opposite was probably true, and that removing the chumming activity from this equation would *increase* the danger of an attack, not reduce it; that the attacks would likely *not* have taken place if dive operators had been working in the area on the days in question (which was not the case during any of the attacks).

I admit that at first glance this statement sounds absolutely crazy, but consider the available evidence and the deductions that can be made from that evidence.

A key factor in this sort of scenario is the composition of the chumming mixtures in common use. Contrary to common belief, shark chum is not a smelly mixture of rotten fish guts and blood but typically consists of ingredients like fresh crushed sardines, anchovy oil and seawater. This is ladled out at a rate of about a quarter-litre every five to seven minutes and almost always creates a well-defined surface slick of about two metres wide which slowly drifts downstream from the boat.

The moment a white shark crosses this slick an instinctive reaction kicks in which it cannot resist. Its highly developed sense of smell and sensory organs control its behaviour from that point, and as a result it always reacts in a very specific manner by swimming directly towards the source of the chum. This is no different from the behaviour of most land-based predators, which instinctively stalk by smell.

The result is that once the shark has picked up the scent of a potential food source – in this case the chum – it is almost impossible for it to swim in the opposite direction because its instincts compel it to move towards where the scent is strongest.

On the occasion of each attack the wind direction was south-southeasterly, meaning it was blowing the water shorewards, and if a dive operator had been in the vicinity his chum slick would have been going the same way.

Now, if a chum slick is drifting in the direction of bathers and surfers in a given area and a white shark was cruising in between them, by far the likeliest scenario is that the shark would keep moving single-mindedly towards the source of the slick and would not peel off en route to attack a human in the shallows. If a shark does not respond to the slick *it is not hungry, and therefore would not be a threat to the surfers and bathers.*

This is not mere theorising but a distillation of 25 years of hands-on experience. I have chummed for white sharks on more than 5 000 occasions, and my success in attracting them to the boat has been virtually 100 per cent. There is no special knack involved here: each and every dive operator, shark researcher and great white shark hunter in the world uses this very same technique and has the same sort of success rate.

In all my years of chumming for white sharks I have never seen or heard of one of them swimming downstream from the source of a chum slick. Nor have I witnessed or heard of a white shark approaching a chum slick from the bow of the boat, the opposite end of the flow.

If the prevailing wind is onshore it would be unlikely to attract a white shark from the open ocean into the area between the boat and the beach. Conversely, any white shark roaming between the source of the chum slick and the beach would almost certainly be compelled by its instincts to move in the direction of the boat and the chum.

The experienced dive operator, therefore, would actually be acting in the bathers' and swimmers' interests by attracting the shark away from them.

There is another aspect to this scenario that provides a built-in safety factor. Once a white shark has been attracted to the dive operator's boat, it is usually easy to keep it there for extended periods; this creates a window of opportunity during which steps can be taken to clear the bathers and surfers while the shark is otherwise occupied.

The case of Gansbaai on the Cape's west coast provides very significant circumstantial evidence in support of my contention. It is a very popular holiday destination, with surfing and swimming obviously being the main attractions. At the same time Gansbaai has more chumming activity than any other place in the world, with eight operators working close inshore on a daily basis all year round. But to date there has not been a single white shark attack in the area, whereas it would surely have been the complete opposite if there was actually a link between chumming and attacks.

Now, I am most emphatically not suggesting that white shark operators should be allowed to ply their trade in and around bathing and surfing areas. But the mythical link between chumming and attacks needs to be exploded, and people should also be made aware of the fact that it is quite easy to remove white sharks from the vicinity of surfing and bathing activities.

Having addressed the chumming issue, the next question that needs to be asked is why there is so much white shark activity in False Bay, and there are several contributing factors that have to be taken into account.

One is the strict white shark protection laws which have been in place since 1991. When this law was passed there was no scientific proof that white sharks were endangered, but the regulations were enacted as a pre-emptive measure to establish the population dynamics of the species.

If we assume that there was a moderately healthy shark population back then, it is safe to assume that there has been a fair population explosion of sharks after almost two decades of unhindered breeding.

Another factor is that for many years False Bay produced large quantities of shoal fish, which resulted in a healthy food chain on which the predators existed. Many people would try to argue that there is quite a substantial seal population in the bay that the great white sharks could feed on, but the fact is that the Cape fur seals are pretty slippery characters, so that a shark often expends massive amounts of energy trying – but failing – to catch one.

Another possible factor seems to be that the Seal Island area is getting a bit crowded (in recent years I have observed up to ten white sharks in this area at one time), and the social hierarchy and pecking order of these complex creatures might also be a reason why they are ranging further into the bay.

Yet another possible factor is that when the prevailing south-southeasterly winds blow onshore in the summer months the activities of the fishing fleet operating out of Kalk Bay result in a massive, uncontrolled chum slick being trapped for days in this corner of the bay. It is a reasonable assumption that when the fishing boats return to harbour, pumping large volumes of fish blood and bits of sardine from their bilges, any white shark in the area will lock on to this very strong stimulus.

The final possible factor is humankind itself. In recent years, recreational water users have multiplied many times and have acquired the means of going further and further out into the ocean, the ancient domain of the white shark. This being the case, it stands to reason that contact between sharks and people is bound to occur more frequently.

Some people have taken to describing False Bay as 'the shark-attack capital of the world'. Well, one is tempted to agree when one considers the alarming numbers (relatively speaking) of white shark attacks on humans and the large number of sightings in recent years. What is extremely disturbing, though, is that although sharks are commonly sighted in and around the popular beaches in this area, the authorities and the life-saving clubs can do very little about it, other than close the affected beach or beaches for a short period.

But go back to the first few years of increased attacks. As a white shark champion I was very concerned about the increase in the number of attacks, so I contacted the authorities to volunteer my services, suggesting that I try a method I had evolved, which consisted of chumming the sharks away from the beaches. But this suggestion fell on deaf ears, and I didn't take the matter any further.

Then, almost exactly a year later, Donovan (who was skippering *Shark Aholic* at the time) telephoned me early one evening to tell me that the beach at Fish Hoek had been cleared on three occasions during the day after a large white shark had been spotted near by.

I decided there and then that I could not stand by and do nothing. I got on the line to the MCM offices in order to tell them that I planned to take action and to ask for their cooperation and blessing, but I was being a bit overoptimistic, since it was Boxing Day and naturally no one was available to take my call. So I decided to go ahead on my own and smooth out any hassles when the MCM offices reopened.

I got up early the next morning and headed for Simon's Town, determined to put my theories to the test and remove the danger by scaring the shark right away from the beaches where it had been spreading alarm and despondency the day before.

Eugene and Donovan were quite surprised by my unannounced arrival, but they were even more surprised when I assembled them and the seven guests who were booked in for a dive trip off Seal Island, described what had happened the previous day and told them of my desire to eliminate the potential danger of a shark attack.

I told the clients that if they agreed to be diverted to this self-imposed task they would not be able to cage dive, but they would still be able to observe and interact with the shark if it made an appearance, and at the same time they would be rendering an important service to their fellow human beings.

The clients weren't over the moon about missing out on the cage dive, but they agreed that if we were able to eliminate the potential shark attack danger, while at the same time coming into contact with a white shark, it was okay with them. That was all I wanted to hear.

When we arrived off Fish Hoek beach around quarter past nine I was disappointed to see that there was a fleet of about ten commercial fishing boats lying directly abreast of it. My concern was that the large and uncontrolled chum slick generated by their activities would interfere with our effort to attract the shark to our boat, so I moved to a spot about 500 metres to the Muizenberg side of the boats and about two and a half kilometres off Kalk Bay harbour.

We anchored and started chumming; there was a moderate to fresh southerly wind blowing directly shoreward, and we soon had a well-defined slick drifting in a straight line towards the harbour adjoining the beach. But nothing happened for about two hours. Then one of our guests, an Irishman, suddenly shouted: 'Shark, I see a shark! Oh, my gosh, I see two sharks out there!'

'Where's the shark?' I demanded, as everyone jumped up and started craning necks in all directions. 'Over there,' he said, pointing in the general direction of the beach, in line with the stern, 'I saw these two fins pop out the water back there, about 500 yards away!'

I asked him how far apart the fins were, and he said two or three metres. I told him that what he had actually seen were the dorsal and tail fins of a single white shark, and that if his estimate of the distance between them was accurate, we could have one about four metres long working its way up the slick toward us. Naturally this didn't do anything to make the excitement abate.

But for the next 20 minutes the shark, if there was a shark, was conspicuous by its absence, and everyone on board settled down to ragging our unfortunate Irish friend. Except me – I had a good idea of what to expect and so kept my eyes on the bait trailing off the stern. And sure enough, after another five or so minutes my pulse began to race as the shark's majestic shape, four metres long if it was an inch, came gliding into view directly behind the floating bait.

My sudden change of body language must have alerted the others, because without a word they all followed my gaze and drank up the magnificent spectacle as the shark cruised close by.

Now we could take the appropriate action, and I mean 'appropriate'. We had come here specifically to confront the shark and get it out of the area, but this could not be done by means of violence or aggression. The law forbade that sort of approach, but in any case I would not have had it any other way even if I had had a free hand: the shark's stunning beauty and its absolute grace and power made me want to admire and observe it, rather than inflict harm.

I instructed Donovan to keep working the bait-line to make sure the shark stayed near the boat, then told the very happy and excited clients that what I wanted to do was keep this one interested while we continued chumming to see if there was a second in the vicinity. This suited them very well, and we continued chumming for another hour, making sure to keep our 'customer' contented in the meantime by allowing it to take three of the four tuna heads we had on board.

When it was clear that there wasn't a second shark in the vicinity I decided to get on with the second phase of my plan and told Donovan to keep the shark busy with our remaining tuna head for a few more minutes before we started coaxing it further out to sea.

Donovan's efforts to tantalise the shark nearly came to a bad end when his attention wandered for a moment and it grabbed the tuna head. This was a potential disaster because the bait had an important role in our final manoeuvre, and for a few seconds the two of them were involved in a splashing and thrashing tug-of-war before he got the tuna head out of the shark's jaws.

Our wildly excited guests weren't too pleased when I told them that we were now going to try to swing the shark out towards the open ocean and scare it off, but Theo the Shark Hunter now assumed the mantle of Theo the Bad Guy, and I told Eugene to start packing away the bits and pieces in preparation for the final phase, in which we would lure the shark out to sea and then send it on its way with a bucketful of a special mixture which was both a chum neutraliser and a strong deterrent.

At this stage a helicopter suddenly came zooming over us. I waved it off, worried that the noise and disturbance would scare the shark into heading the wrong way. It seemed to get the message and banked away towards land, while I took the boat slowly out to sea, throttling down every 50 metres or so to make sure the shark stayed with us.

After about 15 minutes we had opened the gap with the beach by a further 400 or 500 metres, and I slowly turned the boat so that the bow ended up facing the shore, while Donovan kept working the bait's line to make sure the shark stayed astern.

Once we were in position I told Eugene to pour the chum neutralizer into the water, then pull in the line. The shark followed close behind the bait, but when it reached the neutraliser mixture it spun around, thrashed the water with its tail and then shot off in the general direction of the middle of the bay.

Happily I opened the throttles and swung around to go home; I had accomplished my mission and our guests had had an unusual and exciting introduction to the world of the white shark, which had been at least as much fun as diving in a cage. But my happiness faded a little when a Namakurra patrol boat of the South African Navy came out, passed us and then swung around and started closing in behind us, right up our wake.

Oh, bugger me, what the hell is this about? I thought. I could not believe it; it felt as if the damned Navy, police or MCM came charging out after me just about every time I climbed on my boat. I got on the radio to ask the Namakurra's skipper what the problem was. He ignored my question and instructed me to follow him to the naval base. I replied that I needed to disembark my clients at the boat club and suggested he should follow me there, to which he agreed.

Two policemen were waiting when we tied up at our jetty, and the senior one, an inspector, asked to see my dive permit. I showed it him, and after studying it he handed it back, saying that it was in order and that he was sorry to have troubled us.

I asked him what it was all about and he said someone had reported that we had been illegally cage diving with white sharks in the Fish Hoek beach area. I shrugged it off and forgot about it, but next morning the inspector called back and said Marine Coastal Management had instructed him to open a criminal inquiry against me, and asked whether I could come to his office to make a statement.

Totally stunned, not to say distinctly pissed off, I thought: *Oh, shit, here we go again.* A call to MCM didn't bring much clarity. It wasn't actually a police investigation, I was told. It was just to get to the bottom of the complaint that had been received. But this was something of an understatement, because when I had given the inspector my statement the next day he served me with a seizure notice on my boat and said that MCM had instructed him to notify the Navy to apprehend me if I attempted to put to sea and also to inform the False Bay Yacht Club to report to him if I tried to use my boat.

That was the last straw, and I blew up in no uncertain terms. What had I done that was illegal? This was a load of crap! This was a classic case of killing the messenger, of course, since he was only following instructions, and I learned something interesting when things calmed down enough for us to begin chatting.

He turned on his computer and pulled up some photographs of large white sharks swimming very near to the beach. When I asked if they had succeeded in chasing the sharks back to open water, he said: 'No, it's a waste of time. Every time we rush the shark with the boat it simply dives and pops up again about 20 metres away.'

The chumming method I had described in my statement, he added, sounded like a sensible way of doing it (damn right it was – when I spoke to the lifeguards at the beach a few days later, they assured me that the shark we had chased away had not been seen there again).

On that amicable note we parted, and MCM then gave me back my boat and permission to continue working – no explanation, no apology. That was not the end of it, though, because the media picked up on this episode and for the next week or so had a field day with it.

There was, however, a rather ludicrous addendum to this farcical affair when the BBC picked up the story and called me from London that evening for a ten-minute interview: 140 people million around the world would be listening to me stating my case, they said.

At first things went well, with the presenter letting me have my say without much interference. But then he suddenly changed his tactics by swinging the interview around to the hysterical and inaccurate reporting that had raged in the South African media.

Would my activities that day not have ended up conditioning the shark's behaviour? I answered this well-worn question with a simple 'no', to which he came back with: 'Well, I have a gold-fish in a bowl at home, and he has become so used to me that he knows that when I tap on the glass it's feeding time and without fail he comes to me.'

My answer wasn't all that tactful. 'You're missing the point completely,' I said. 'The glass bowl that I work in is one hell of a lot bigger than yours. You most certainly had to tap the glass of your goldfish bowl many times to condition your fish in its very tiny world, to cover the few inches to your hand. I, on the other hand, tapped only once on the vast glass of the ocean to attract the shark. That's why I'm confident that no conditioning took place.'

I didn't know it just then, but my conversations with sharks were nearly over. In February 2003 I received a letter from MCM, informing me that my dive exemption had been withdrawn with immediate effect. Why? They didn't say, I didn't know and I was not given an opportunity to state my case. I can only assume that I was the victim of politics and controversy that were way beyond my level and my ability to handle.

Though angry and bitterly disappointed, I took stock and decided to call it quits. I had had a long run and done some worthwhile things, and I just didn't feel inclined to get involved in more soul-draining struggles.

And that, finally, was it for me.

As I look back on my shark-hunting days, I reflect on my past with no regret or feeling of shame about my actions. Rather, I look upon this period of my life as part of a learning pro-cess from which a more complete and informed individual has evolved. And I feel very privileged to have been afforded the opportunity to learn from and interact with these complex and mighty creatures on their terms.

Sure, they attack and kill humans from time to time. But we have to remember that they are wild creatures, both living and hunting in their own environment, just like their land-based counterparts such as the lion and tiger. That's why I would rather coexist with these mighty creatures and learn from them than fear or hunt them.

I am disappointed not by the white sharks but by another species altogether, *Homo sapiens*. I have always believed in working and interacting with others in an atmosphere of mutual honour, respect and dignity, and it's sad to have to admit that it has been difficult to live up to this somewhat naive philosophy. On the other hand, my negative experiences have actually strengthened my resolve and my belief in what I stood and fought for.

Thus I might be a little battered and bruised, but I'm still willing to put myself on the line if the need arises and my misgivings are proved to be wrong. The great white shark's well-being and future existence come first with me, and if the various role-players in the arena want me to join hands with them in the conservation and management of the species, they will find me willing and ready.

In a way, I spoke my own epitaph some time ago when a close friend asked me if I would be willing to do it all over again.

'Hell, yes,' I said, 'you can bet your life on it. I'd do it all over again, and take all the crap and abuse that comes with it with a smile on my face. It's been one hell of a roller-coaster ride, but I would sure as hell be willing to pay a very high price to go on it again.'

So I would like to end my story by saying thanks once more to all the people who believed in me and supported me during half a lifetime of adventure, in good times and bad alike. And, in particular, I want to thank those amazing sea creatures who let me ride on their magic carpet and turned me into a better and more fulfilled person. As I continue to say, I am a very privileged individual indeed.

This is not to say that I have withdrawn from the world. There's still a lot of life in me and a lot of adrenaline that hasn't been burned up yet, and the blue water stretches as widely as it ever did. Who knows – perhaps the sharkaholic will make a comeback one day ...

Epilogue: The science of the journey

Craig Ferreira

While my father and Len Compagno were fighting for the honour of the white shark, I had the best job in the world. I was operations officer of the WSRP and was responsible for the field research unit, a small team of dedicated men and women with our 22-foot research vessel, our towing vehicle and the equipment we used while working with the sharks.

Usually there were three of us in the field team at any one time, and my team was primarily Chris Fellows, Rob Lawrence and Liam Reynolds. These were top guys who not only got on with the job but were also a hoot to be around, so we never had a dull moment.

I would be told that I had to go down to Gansbaai or Struisbaai or Mossel Bay or wherever to work on one project or another. We would saddle up with all of our equipment and disappear into the wild world of the white shark for weeks, even months, at a time. Our days would be taken up with tagging sharks, taking tissue samples from them, attaching cameras to them, diving with them, filming them and recording data. Evenings were spent at the local pub, drinking beer and playing pool. Life could not have been better.

I was really privileged to work cheek by jowl with sharks for at least nine months of each year, and during those times we did some really good and interesting work. As early as 1992, Chris and I were free diving with white sharks; we tagged around 500 and we were the first people in the world to attach cameras to them and extract their blood for analysis. We worked on a number of DNA projects and took part in the making of some incredible documentaries.

None of this could have taken place but for the hard and grinding work my father put in, not to mention Len, my sisters Tracy and Cherie, and all the other people who joined our cause.

My particular interest in white sharks centres on their social behaviour, and I have had the opportunity to spend so much time with them in their own environment that I feel I have gained a very good insight into their ways. That is why my father asked me to make contributions to this book, so that I could share some of what I have learnt. And because learning was what it was all about, it has been a pleasure to share what I have seen, done and discovered to date.

I should add that although we have learnt a great deal about the white shark over the past 17 years, there is still much that we don't know. I have reached the point where I am quite content with the fact that the white shark still guards its secrets, and I think this is part of its allure for me. The white shark is a constant challenge to us and I truly believe that it always will be.

I have my ideas and theories. Some I consider to be based on fact and others are closely related to factual evidence. And I am always ready to debate my theories and ideas, and possibly build on them. But I would certainly not be foolish enough to consider myself an expert on all aspects of the white shark. There is no such thing, and this is not going to change in a hurry.

Everything you ever wanted to know about great white sharks

As my son Craig notes in the Epilogue to our narrative, there is no such thing as an expert on the great white shark. In many ways it remains as mysterious a creature as it was in the days when the *Jaws* mentality ruled the world. But two decades of research and experience by scientists and rough-and-ready enthusiasts like Craig and myself, and the rest of our team, Tracy, Cherie, Liam, Kim, Chris, Rob and Nico, have allowed a modest body of knowledge to start accumulating. This part of my book is dedicated to passing on some of the knowledge acquired by our team of dedicated shark enthusiasts.

As Craig has been lucky enough to have spent so much time in the field, it seems appropriate that he should the be the one to answer a number of what are now known as 'Frequently Asked Questions'.

VITAL STATISTICS
Anyone who is interested in great white sharks should know something about their vital statistics – how big they can grow, what they eat, how they reproduce and so on – if only to filter out some of the most misleading myths and legends. This is not easy because there is still so much about them that we have yet to discover, but we do know enough to get the reader off to a good start.

How big can a great white shark grow?
The great white shark is the largest predatory shark in the ocean, but the maximum size the species can attain is still a matter for some debate. Based on personal observation of the largest one I ever saw, my old protagonist the Submarine, a great white shark can reach at least seven metres and weigh between 3 000 and 4 000 kilograms.

This sounds a trifle excessive – it is longer than three very tall men lying head-to-foot, after all – but it is not a wild guess. It will be remembered how the Submarine came right up to our 5.5-metre boat and spent quite a bit of time with us, so that we were able to make an accurate estimation of its size.

In my opinion, though, the normal maximum size is probably around six metres. The Submarine was far larger than any other white shark we have ever encountered, but there are exceptions to the rule in any species, *Homo sapiens* included, and till evidence to the contrary is produced I will believe that the Submarine was one of them.

On average, however, female white sharks grow to around five metres in length at maturity, which takes them about 15 years to reach. Male sharks reach maturity in about eight years, at which stage they will usually be between 3.5 metres and 3.6 metres long. The average size of the sharks along the Cape coast was about 3.4 metres overall, while sharks in Natal's waters averaged about 2.7 metres.

How do you measure a great white shark in the sea?

Not with a tape measure, that's for sure. We tried to log the size of each white shark we encountered during our study period, and we became quite accurate at estimating their length.

One useful tool was the tags we planted in them, which were exactly 70 mm long and very visible. We would frequently obtain good photographs of these tags attached to the backs of their involuntary hosts and then use them to work out the exact length of the sharks concerned. When we compared the results with our estimations they were usually very close.

In 1995, incidentally, we were concerned to spot very few young of that year and even fewer adult females. But this seems to have changed for the better over the past ten years, and today we are encountering far more young of the year and, over certain periods, some very big adults.

Where do they occur and how deep can they go?
Great white sharks are true cosmopolitans – they can be found just about everywhere in the oceans of the world. They are listed as inshore predators that occur along the continental shelves and in shallow bays, but having said that, white sharks have been sighted hundreds of kilometres out to sea and readily travel from continent to continent across vast tracts of ocean.

The white shark is primarily a temperate-water inhabitant, with major population groups congregating off the southern coast of South Africa, California and South Australia, often near large seal colonies like the ones on the Farralon Islands of California, along the Cape coast of South Africa and off South Australia. However, they also readily penetrate tropical oceans and have been known to venture deep into very cold regions. White shark sightings have been reported from latitudes of 54 degrees, both north and south.

They seem to spend most of their time near the surface, but have been known to swim to depths of hundreds of metres; the deepest dives recorded so far are close to 1 000 metres.

What do they eat?
They are macro-predators, meaning they can – and do – kill and consume anything smaller than they are. Young white sharks, which are around a metre in length at birth, have long narrow teeth which are designed to feed on fish and other small prey such as the smaller shark species, squid and so on. Then, as the sharks grow larger, their teeth widen out to become more blade-like and they adapt to taking on larger prey such as seals, dolphins, tuna and turtles. White sharks also feed on carrion such as whale carcasses.

Are they cold-blooded like other fish?
Great whites are actually warm-blooded, in the sense that their body temperatures are higher than the ambient temperature of

the water around them. The well-known shark scientist Ken Goldman found that free-swimming white sharks maintained a body temperature of about 25 degrees Celsius, even when the ambient water temperature fluctuated.

Their body temperature is probably elevated because their normal prey animals, such as seals, dolphin and game fish, are all rather fast movers. A steady elevated body temperature would keep their muscles warm so that the shark would be ready to pounce on any prey animal and catch it, even when it was fleeing at top speed.

Are white sharks affected by water temperature?

Since white sharks are primarily temperate-water animals but will readily penetrate both tropical and polar-region waters, a question we sought an answer to during our researches was whether local water temperatures had an influence on the movements of great whites.

During our five-year project we worked in water temperatures ranging from 11 to 23 degrees Celsius and found white sharks across the entire temperature range. We noticed, however, a significant drop in the number of sharks in the colder temperatures, but we still do not know whether it was the temperature itself, the effect of the temperature on sightings or other factors such as the lack of fish in cold water or diminished seal activity.

How well can they see?

White sharks have quite large eyes surrounded by substantial muscles, and so have great eyesight. Their eyes are also particularly light-sensitive, which allows them to see very well in poor light or dirty water. In this sense their eyes are like underwater video cameras. When you record underwater and then view the tape, the water always seems to be clearer on the monitor because the camera is more light-sensitive than your eyes. The same applies to sharks.

Observation shows that vision is an important sense to white sharks. They use their eyes to inspect objects, and when hunting will actually lift their heads above the water in order to inspect surface objects (we call this the 'spy hop'). If they didn't have good eyesight, why would they bother doing this?

The placement of the white shark's eyes provides another important clue to their importance. The shark's eyes are located above the jaws, very close to its snout. This places the eyes very close to where all the action is, but also makes them vulnerable because of the shark's method of feeding, and so they have built-in protection.

When a big white shark feeds on a 500-kilo seal, it bites into the ribcage and then shakes its prey violently from side to side. The ribs break, the seal's body opens up and the shark pushes its jaw and head further into the carcass to pull it apart. The broken ribs are all around the shark's face; as sharp as razors, they could easily puncture the shark's eye – but they don't, because of two built-in safety features.

Most species have what is called a nictitating membrane, which is like an eyelid that covers the eyes when the shark wants to protect them. The nictitating membrane is not enough to protect a white shark's eyes from its robust feeding habits, however, and so the entire eye can be rolled backwards into its deep socket. As it sinks back, the eye depresses and exposes a layer of tough tissue. This is why a shark's eye sometimes appears to have gone white.

Out of all the thousands of great whites we have worked with over the years we have only spotted two with damaged eyes, proof that this protective system works very well.

How keen is their sense of smell?

A shark has a very acute sense of smell and can detect even tiny dilutions of fish juice or blood in the water. This does not mean that a shark can smell everything around it. If a whale is bleeding in the water sharks will not automatically come cruising in from all directions; they would have to swim through an odour trail before smelling the whale's blood.

It is like a man walking past a bakery. He will only smell the bread baking if he is downwind; if he is upwind he will smell absolutely nothing. The same goes for sharks, except that they have an amazing ability to detect miniscule amounts of water-odour, and the hungrier they are, the better their sense of smell. Scientific tests have shown that very hungry sharks can smell dilutions of one part fish blood in millions and even billions of parts of water.

Can they hear?

Sharks have two ways of detecting sounds. They have an ear on the top of the head with which they probably hear in the same way as terrestrial animals, but they also have another way of hearing: the lateral line.

This is a line of small pressure sensors running down the length of each side of the body, which detects minute pressure-waves in the water. The sensors enable a shark to detect a fish or animal struggling in the water, determine its size and work out how far away it is. It is even possible, although no one knows for certain, that a shark is capable of detecting the heartbeat of a large animal.

What are the ampullae of Lorenzini?

The ampullae of Lorenzini around a shark's snout and mouth make up the most amazing sensory systems found in nature. They look like small spots or pores, but are actually little tubules or canals filled with a jelly-like substance that has electrical properties similar to a semiconductor.

Through this highly acute system sharks can pick up minute bioelectric currents emitted by other animals; if a shark is hunting rays that are buried under the sand it will employ the ampullae to detect them in much the same way as a mine detector sniffs out landmines.

It is even possible (although this remains to be proven) that they can detect the earth's magnetic fields and use them for navigation, and recent research suggests that they might allow sharks to detect changes in water temperature.

It is estimated that a shark's awareness of electrical outputs is 50 million times more sensitive than our own. To place this into some perspective, imagine taking a normal penlight battery and then hooking it up to a shark by means of a wire that is 1 600 kilometres long. The shark would be able to pick up the battery's 1.5-volt discharge.

How do their teeth and jaws work?

Sharks have an amazing jaw and tooth system, which allows them always to have a beautiful set of pearly whites. A shark's jaw is actually made up of cartilage, and not bone, and is not part of the skeleton but a separate entity that is directly connected to a mass of muscle.

Normally, a shark's jaw is tucked away under its snout, which helps to make it highly hydrodynamic. At first glance this arrangement might seem inefficient for the purposes of feeding because the snout would get in the way, but thanks to its construction, a shark that is about to feed can use the surrounding muscles to thrust its jaw forward.

This changes the shape of the head quite noticeably and, of course, reduces its hydrodynamic efficiency, but at that point a little extra drag is not important – what is needed is killing ability – and when it has caught and eaten its prey the jaw slides back again as easily as it went forward.

Because the jaw is made of cartilage rather than bone it is quite flexible, and I believe that this flexibility is of great importance in the case of large sharks taking on large prey. If a 1 000-kilo white shark attacks a 500-kilo seal at 30 kilometres an hour, its jaw has to absorb great stress at the moment of impact, but it will not fracture as it might do if it were solid bone.

Sharks' teeth are just as amazing. A shark might grow old but it will always have a sharp and functional set of teeth in its mouth, even though they are subjected to great wear and tear – large prey, like seals, possess strong bones that have to be bitten through, and it is not uncommon for a shark tearing up a big seal to dislodge or break some of its teeth.

Sharks have multiple rows of teeth. The white shark has a single row of teeth at the front of the top jaw that it uses to carve and cut sections of tissue away, and two or three rows of narrower ones in the bottom jaw, which are used to lock on to the prey. Behind these rows of functional teeth are several rows of dormant teeth, the rearmost only partly developed, which mostly lie flat and are not used while feeding.

Sharks' teeth never stop growing, and as the front row of dormant teeth mature, they slowly push at the functional teeth till the latter are dislodged during feeding or simply fall out ('teeth shedding', as we call it). The fully-developed dormant teeth then move up to fill the gap. A shark may go through as many as 20 000 teeth during its life.

How much does a white shark eat?

This is a question for which we have no conclusive answer. Some scientists say that a white shark can survive for a very long period on one large meal, perhaps as much as two months, while others say that they eat all the time. I can only comment on the basis of personal experience and make logical deductions from that experience.

White sharks have large stomachs and the ability to consume large amounts of food. I have seen obviously well-fed, quite rotund 4.8-metre-long white sharks consume an entire 250-kilo seal within a matter of minutes, and I have seen others gorge to such an extent on a dead whale that they could hardly move.

This leads me to believe that the white shark is a very opportunistic feeder and will eat even when its stomach is full – a natural survival instinct in the world of free-ranging animals, whose denizens never know when the next meal will come along.

Then again, it is simple common sense to conclude that a great white shark that weighs 1 000 kilos or so and has an elevated body temperature of 25 degrees Celsius will require large amounts of food to sustain its energy levels.

How do they reproduce?

Little is known about white sharks' mating and reproduction, but there is a basic understanding which derives not only from research on other shark species but also my personal observations of a number of pregnant white sharks I caught during my hunting days.

White sharks take a long time to become sexually mature, and they grow slowly. Currently, the only way to determine if a female really is sexually mature is if you cut her open and find she is pregnant. With males it is easier, because they have what are known as 'claspers', or external sexual organs. If the claspers are rigid and calcified, the shark is mature.

White shark courtship remains an unexplored field, but some indications may be gained from observing other shark species and examining females for 'love-bites' around her head and on her pectoral fins. A female that has been courted will have many small love-bites.

White sharks are internally fertilised and so copulate in the same way as mammals. The male who gains the female's favour uses his teeth to hold gently on to the female's pectoral fins while they mate. The gestation period, we believe, might be somewhere between one and two years, during which each pup feeds off a large attached sac of yolk; a little later, when the pups are ready to start eating, the mother will continue to produce yolks for them, which scientists call 'oophagy', or uterine cannibalism.

A female normally carries between seven and 14 pups, and when they reach term they are born fully formed, measuring anything between a metre and 1.3 metres long. A female does not suckle her young; the young sharks are born ready to hunt and fend for themselves.

Sex ratios

In our study we recorded the genders of the white sharks and came up with some interesting results. Firstly, the occurrence of males and females changed during the year. At certain times we would only sight females, at other times only males, and then there were periods where there was a mix of the sexes.

Overall, we found that in Cape waters the ratio of males to females was 1:3.4. This differed from the mix of animals taken in the shark nets of KwaZulu-Natal, where the ratio was one male to 1.4 females.

Are white sharks seasonal?

No, they are not, or at least not along the South African coast. For five years we worked during every month of the year, and although there were fluctuations in shark numbers from day to day (as noted elsewhere), the white sharks were present during the entire period.

WHITE SHARK BEHAVIOUR

Great whites' behaviour is a complicated subject with many grounds for debate. Yet it is a very important subject because it flies in the face of many popular perceptions. Most people see the white shark as a simple killing machine, but it is a complex animal with equally complex social behaviour.

In this connection, it is vital to remember that most of what we see occurs on or near the surface of the ocean, and because the white shark spends the greater part of its life below the surface we are only observing a very small part of its behaviour.

So I am going to present a general overview based on personal observation, research, discussion, common sense and gut feeling, leaving the reader free to debate my ideas and theories.

Are they the lonely lords of the sea?

The general perception is that the white sharks are antisocial loners, but our observations indicate that they are often found in groups, frequently congregate in specific areas and seem to move around together.

Between 1990 and 1997 we tagged about 600 white sharks along the southern African coastline between False Bay and Mossel Bay, and in the process were rewarded with some very interesting observations and results.

For example, we would tag sharks A and B in Gansbaai on a particular day. Several months later we would sight them again on the same day at Struisbaai, about 100 kilometres further along the coast. On other occasions we would observe sharks A, B, C, D and E at Dyer Island on one particular day, and then several weeks later we would encounter sharks A,B and E there on the same day. The inevitable conclusion is that certain sharks move around together for periods of time.

In 1993 we spent the entire year working at Struisbaai, and during one three-week period we observed white sharks moving as a group on what resembled a rigid timetable. We would be chumming and baiting from seven o'clock in the morning; around two o'clock in the afternoon, the sharks would arrive in a group. This happened day after day. No matter how long we had been chumming, the sharks would arrive within minutes of two o'clock. It was so precise that eventually we amused ourselves by betting on the exact time of their arrival.

The logical deduction we made was that the sharks were moving as a group through some kind of cycle. The nature of the cycle? Well, that was just another of the many things we didn't know about the white sharks then, and still don't.

Who's the boss?

Great white sharks have a distinct hierarchical structure that is based on size, with smaller specimens knowing their place in the pecking order. If three white sharks of different sizes are feeding off a single large seal carcass, for example, the largest shark will have first access, the second largest will come next and the smallest will wait till last to take what is left, or suffer the consequences.

Posturing

Posturing is something similar to the behaviour of two dogs sizing each other up, strutting with their tails up in the air, the message being that they do not particularly want to fight but are willing to do so. What usually happens then is that either one of the dogs signals submission or they get to grips.

The same sort of thing is seen in a number of shark species and involves the shark concerned pushing its pectoral fins down and sometimes arching its back. I have never seen white sharks arch their backs, but they will frequently push their pectoral fins down by way of warning.

Posturing usually takes place between two white sharks of similar size. A typical posturing situation involves two sharks of similar size who both want first access to a prey item. Usually the posturing works and the more aggressive or committed shark wins the standoff.

Gaping

Gaping is an escalation of posturing. If posturing does not solve a dispute about who gets first bite at a prey item, one or other of the sharks will gape at the other by opening its mouth in a threatening manner. There are different degrees of gaping. It can be relatively passive or quite aggressive, with the shark thrusting its jaw forward, once or several times.

The face-off

A face-off situation occurs when two sharks swim towards each other and then both back off when they are about a metre apart. What is interesting about this is that they do not swim directly towards one another but always converge at an angle.

The aim of this, we have concluded, is to avoid accidental contact. If they converge at an angle, each shark has only one direction of retreat, namely away from the other shark. If they went at each other head to head there would always be the possibility that they might break in the same direction and collide.

Violent and nonviolent behaviour

A popular perception is that great white sharks are very violent animals and will attack one another if they can. The truth is that they are exceptionally calm and controlled creatures that go to great lengths to avoid fighting.

Much of their behaviour is aimed at avoiding physical contact. It is quite common for a terrestrial animal to take on a larger one in combat and win, but with white sharks it is just the opposite. They do not use combat as a means of establishing dominance, and in fact one very rarely sees a white shark striking another, or one with combat wounds.

There is an instinctive logic in this behaviour. A white shark is such a formidable killing machine that it can inflict massive damage on an opponent very quickly; therefore it would be very destructive for them to go around hammering one another. But their way of establishing dominance by nonaggressive means raises a very interesting question: how does one white shark know that it is larger or smaller than another? One deduction is that they must have some kind of self-awareness.

Sharing

During lectures on white shark behaviour, I have been asked whether they will share prey. Well, when they feed off a large dead whale, they have to share, and they do. And when the prey is smaller? I recall a typical case of such prey-sharing we observed at Dyer Island in 1993.

A large, obviously ailing female seal swam from Geyser Rock towards our boat, and as she arrived a huge great white shark attacked and killed her with its first bite. At this time two other white sharks were in the area, both smaller than the attacker.

The large shark fed on the seal for a while and then backed off; the second-largest of the others took its place and after a while gave way to the smallest shark. This process continued till the entire seal had been devoured.

It should be remembered, however, that although such calm, systematic sharing of smaller prey appears to be the rule, there are always exceptions. For example, if the attacker had been very hungry it might well have consumed the entire seal.

WHITE SHARK ATTACKS
The white shark is a wonderful and beautiful creature, and when we watch a wildlife documentary on television and see it take out an elephant seal, our first reaction is to be amazed by its efficiency and power.

But as soon as it attacks a human our attitudes swing right around, and the sleek, awesome ocean predator becomes a bloodthirsty monster who is the enemy of all humankind. Our first instinct is to avenge the attack by reprisals on any sharks large enough to qualify as a possible perpetrator.

I am the first to admit that a shark attack on a human being is a frightening and horrifying thing, and I understand why people take reprisals after one. But the reprisals serve no purpose at all. Sharks are not at war with humankind, any more than they are with the other animals in the sea. Human flesh has no special taste that attracts them. At the risk of being regarded as facetious, a great white's danger to mankind may be summed up as 'meat is meat, and a shark must eat'.

If we accept, then, that the occasional attacks on humans are isolated incidents which are not driven by any higher emotion than simple hunger, the only logical approach is to see the attacks in the right perspective and determine what is necessary to prevent them.

Some people are so paranoid about shark attacks that they never venture into the sea. That is doubly unfortunate, because such people not only deprive themselves of a healthy leisure activity, they never get to explore the wonders and beauty of our oceans.

So if the words below can eliminate at least some of that unwarranted fear – and the hatred that often accompanies it – a great thing will have been achieved.

We are the planet's dominant species. But we are more than that. Dominance goes hand in hand with responsibility and the understanding of subordinate species. So we are guardians as well as masters – and one can hardly be the guardian of a species one does not understand, or even actively hates.

What is a shark attack?

A shark attack is quite simply a shark biting a person, the bites varying from a nip to a fatal strike. The most fortunate survivor of all is he who gets away with nothing more than a chomp out of his surfboard and a few premature grey hairs.

Why do shark attacks occur?

Sharks are predators that inhabit both the deepest and shallowest parts of the oceans, so wherever you are in the oceans of the world, you have a chance of running into them. For the most part, sharks are more afraid of humans than we are of them, and in 99 per cent of cases the shark will have fled long before we are even aware that it was in the vicinity.

Quite simply, attacks occur on the very rare occasions when humans and large predatory sharks encounter one another at close quarters. It is simply a case of a person being in the wrong place at the wrong time. Sharks do not cruise around looking for human prey. In most cases, they simply come upon humans in the water, and if the sharks are large enough and hungry enough, they will attack, probably mistaking humans for their usual prey.

Most sharks kill prey that they can consume, and therefore will usually attack creatures reasonably smaller than themselves. Since most shark species do not attain sizes much above two metres, they will generally not grow large enough to take on humans.

The white shark, on the other hand, grows far larger than two metres in length and consequently is able and willing to attack large prey. A full-grown white shark is capable of attacking and killing prey as large as elephant seals, which might weigh more than 2 000 kilos. For such a shark a human being would be the same size as one of its smaller prey items.

As far as I am concerned the only potentially dangerous sharks, as far as humans are concerned, are the ones that are large enough, have the necessary equipment and occur inshore where humans frequently utilise the water for recreation. The rest are not usually dangerous to humans, and if and when the extremely rare attack occurs, it is as much a freak accident as being hit by lightning ... although the odds are far smaller.

Which sharks are dangerous to humans?

There are about 500 species of shark in the oceans of the world, and 12 of them are listed as dangerous or potentially dangerous. Even this is a bit misleading, and I will explain why.

The 12 red-flagged species are the great white, tiger, bull, sand tiger, grey reef, dusky, great hammerhead, blue, oceanic white tip, bronze whaler, lemon and sandbar sharks. This list sounds formidable, but once we bring in some perspective we realise that most of these sharks are quite harmless.

It is true that for a shark to be dangerous it must be large enough for it to see a human being as a smaller and thus weaker prey item, which eliminates nearly all the different shark species. It is also true that members of what one might call the 'Big 12' can grow to a formidable size, much larger than a human being.

But this does not mean that they will attack humans.

Firstly, let us look at the oceanic white tip, blue and great hammerhead sharks. They certainly grow large enough to take on prey the size of humans, but they are all pelagic sharks that inhabit the deep ocean, very far from any bathing beach.

The hammerhead has been known to come quite close to shore on occasion, but in general the only people it would pose a threat to would be survivors of a ship-sinking or aircraft accident far offshore – hardly a frequent occurrence.

This is not to say that they would automatically attack humans even if they did swim close inshore; open-ocean scuba divers frequently dive with them, and in fact many dive companies market excursions with this species.

Secondly, the sand tiger shark has been implicated in some attacks, but these have all been accidents. This shark is often found in the shallows, but they feed on fish and their jaws are not designed for large prey such as humans and similar-sized other mammals.

Sand tigers hunt by swimming along very slowly and then suddenly striking at their prey. On vary rare occasions, a sand tiger finding itself in shallow dirty water might grab a person's foot that suddenly appears in front of it, but it will not hold on once it realises that the foot belongs to a much larger creature. That is why sand tigers are favourites with divers the world over and are generally regarded as harmless.

Thirdly, there is the mako shark. The mako is a superbly built creature that can attain a size of four to five metres, and a large one could certainly attack and kill or fatally wound a human being. But the mako is not designed to attack such prey. It has long, smooth, slender teeth, much like the sand tiger's, which rake backwards into the mouth and are designed for catching small prey such as squid, mackerel and other fish; the teeth hold and trap the prey, which is ripped apart and shredded when the shark shakes its head from side to side.

Fourthly, the dusky, lemon, grey reef, bronze whaler and sandbar sharks are fish-eaters and an attack by any one of them will either be an accident or a result of provocation. Only the large adults of these species could be considered dangerous, but you really do not have to worry, and if you encounter one it would be more afraid of you than the other way around.

The three species that are dangerous to humans are the great white shark, the tiger shark and the bull shark, which account for almost all serious or fatal shark attacks, firstly because they grow large enough to take on prey the size of humans and secondly because they are frequently found near the shoreline – the bull shark in particular will readily venture into shallow water, or even into a river or a lagoon.

The tiger and bull sharks are warm-water animals and will not be found in water cooler than 22 degrees Celsius, while the white shark can be found in both warm and cool water.

Their mouth equipment tells the story. All three species have wide jaws and broad, blade-like teeth, serrated at the edges, which are designed for grabbing on to a large prey item like a dolphin and then cutting large chunks of tissue from it.

How many people do sharks kill every year?

Not many. The dangerous species have many opportunities to attack humans, but they will almost always just keep cruising along, because, like a lion, a shark needs to be in hunting mode before it attacks, and it also prefers to attack prey with which it is familiar.

A shark can differentiate fish from seals, dolphins from fish and humans from any of the others, so in most instances a large shark that chances upon a human in the water realises that what it has encountered is not its normal prey, and just swims off.

Attacks do take place, of course, but in most cases the person survives and often there is little or no loss of tissue. This indicates that, once the shark had realised that what it had attacked was not its usual food, it let go and swam off. Now and again a shark will kill the person concerned, and on rare occasions a very large shark may even consume the victim, but this is not the norm.

In any case, there are about 100 recorded shark attacks worldwide every year, something like 26 per cent of which are fatal. The incidence of shark attacks has increased over the past few decades and this can be attributed to several factors, one of them being the fact that water sports are becoming ever more popular all over the world, so there are more and more humans in the water for more and more reasons. Simple mathematics tells one that the more people there are in the water, the greater the chance of an attack.

Overfishing and habitat degradation may also have a part to play. When humans deplete the shark's natural food and destroy its environment, it may start ranging further away from its traditional hunting areas in search of something to eat. This brings more sharks into contact with people.

Still, the incidence of shark attacks is extremely low, and the chances of the individual being attacked have not really increased. To place this whole matter in perspective one should look at some statistics on fatalities. On an annual basis coconuts kill about 150 people, domestic dogs kill many more people than sharks do, snakes kill 40 000 people, tigers take out about 500 people and so on and so on; what the figures say is that if sharks are really bloodthirsty killers, they are doing a pretty incompetent job.

Where do white shark attacks occur?

Statistics on the exact number of recorded unprovoked white shark attacks worldwide vary somewhat, but a number of sources confirm that almost 51 per cent of all such attacks in the twentieth century occurred along the Pacific coast of the USA, with 67 attacks in California, 11 off Oregon, and two in Washington State. Many of these attacks occurred in an area known as the 'red triangle'.

Some sources show Australia second with 32 attacks, or 20 per cent of the total, while others put South Africa in this position with 59 attacks recorded between 1922 and 1999. New Zealand accounted for 12 attacks (five per cent of the total), with the rest scattered around the world – Hawaii recorded three, Japan five, Chile four, Italy three, Argentina one.

The northernmost recorded attack took place in Puget Sound, Washington State, which lies at latitude 47 degrees 50 minutes, and the southernmost off Campbell Island, New Zealand, at latitude 52 degrees 32 minutes.

At what time of day did these attacks occur?

With only one exception all the attacks took place between six am and six pm, in other words, during the daylight hours. There could be two reasons for this. The first and most obvious is the fact that humans use the waters of the oceans almost exclusively during the daylight hours. Another possible reason is that white sharks do not feed as actively at night.

What was the outcome of the attacks?

It is truly amazing that more deaths have not resulted from recorded attacks by white sharks, given their efficiency at killing their prey. In all the recorded attacks, only 26 per cent resulted in death. There are a number of possible reasons for this; it would require another book to go into this question in detail, but the following main reasons might provide some answers.

Medical rescue and emergency treatment have become highly efficient and effective over the past few decades. This has gone a long way towards reducing the number of fatalities. One look at the statistics proves the point. Prior to the 1950s, 91 percent of white shark attacks ended in death for the victims. During the 1950s, as medical treatment improved, 50 percent of attacks were fatal, and since then, the fatality rate has decreased to only 15 percent.

Although the United States has by far the greatest incidence of white shark attacks, it also has the least number of fatalities (12 out of 102 between 1876 and 1999). This is probably largely due to the fact that medical rescue services in the USA are excellent. However, I believe that there are other reasons over and above excellent medical treatment.

Attacks along the USA's eastern Pacific coastline, including the shores of Washington, Oregon, California and Mexico, present by far the largest case history of white shark attacks, with 71 recorded between 1926 and 1993. In Chile, on the other hand, only four white shark attacks have been recorded, three of them proved fatal. The situation is similar in the Mediterranean, where shark attacks are rare but fatality is almost 70 per cent.

In Australian waters 21 out of 342 recorded white shark attacks have resulted in death, nine of the victims never being recovered. In South Africa there were 59 recorded white shark attacks between 1922 and 1994, of which only ten proved fatal, with five victims unrecovered.

Why are people so scared of sharks?

Many people have a fear of being attacked by a shark that borders on the irrational. If you ask them why, they would probably blame movies such as *Jaws*, *Blue Water*, *White Death* and a host of others. But the truth is that we have feared sharks for as long as we have been entering the sea. The movies and books have served only to compound that fear and make it more thrilling.

'Thrilling'? I use the word deliberately, because I think people actually enjoy it. In my opinion people *like* to be afraid of sharks and make fascinating monsters out of them in their minds. When we climb into our cars or board an aircraft, we do not give dying a second thought unless we have a specific phobia. But when we go for a swim in the ocean, we get hung up by a fear of being eaten alive by a shark.

The fact that statistically we have far more chance of leaving this world in a car or aircraft crash does not seem to make the slightest difference to our unrealistic terror of sharks.

In a year in which there is a high rate of shark attacks worldwide (say about 100), no more than 26 per cent will be fatal. So we are looking at no more than 26 people dying as a result of these attacks, whereas on average 700 000 will die in motor vehicles and 1 500 to 3 000 in air crashes.

Consider, too, how many people enter the water annually – the figure runs into millions. In order to obtain a balanced picture we have to put the frightening prospect of shark attacks into the right perspective. Once we are able to manage this, our fear should be greatly diminished and our pleasure in the ocean much increased.

Why do sharks attack people?

There are several reasons why large predator sharks attack people, some of which are mentioned elsewhere in this section of the book, but they merit repeating.

The most common reason is that the shark is hungry and has mistaken the human for its normal prey. Other reasons could be provocation, such as accidental or intentional confrontation, or defensive behaviour on the part of the shark if it perceives the human as a possible threat. Territorial behaviour could also play a role.

From my many years of interacting with these mighty creatures I am convinced that sharks do not perceive us as 'humans'.

We are simply another species in their environment, and if the shark is hungry and it feels that it has the advantage over its prospective prey, it will attack, just as it will attack any other marine animal of the right size.

Sharks have attacked some divers because the divers have provoked them, either by following them around or by trying to touch them. Large sharks will almost certainly lash out if other creatures come too close or attempt to touch them, both which they perceive as threatening actions. This defensive behaviour usually consists of no more than a warning bite; the irony is that although a warning bite is usually just that – a warning to back off – humans are so fragile that it will quite likely result in serious injury or death.

Mistaken identity is probably the most common cause of attacks on humans. Murky waters near a beach or river-mouth can easily result in accidental encounters when sharks are around. A shark hunting in dirty water might see a human leg in front of it, pick up a food-signal of sorts and seize it, not knowing that it is attached to a human. In cases such as this the shark usually lets go again after the first bite, as if it loses interest once it realises that this life-form is not part of its normal diet.

On the other hand, to a shark patrolling underwater a surfer on his board may look like a seal or turtle, and then it will not hesitate to attack. This was well illustrated in the BBC natural history documentary on white sharks. As an experiment, the biologist Peter Pyle dragged a surfboard through the waters around the Farallon Islands west of the San Francisco coast. Often the white sharks were spurred to immediate action, but quietly investigated and then went on their way. Others, perhaps hungrier ones, would be deceived and launched powerful and very frightening attacks on the boards.

All around the world, divers and spear-fishermen in wetsuits have been attacked by white sharks, but in most cases the sharks have quickly released their grip after the first bite, so that usually the divers have not lost limbs or tissue and have recovered fully. In these cases it is very possible that the white sharks mistook the divers for seals, but let go when they realised their mistake.

The most gruesome type of attack is, of course, the one in which the shark, having identified a swimmer as prey, does *not* let go after the first bite but carries on. This rarely happens, but when it does the results are horrible in the extreme. The victim loses one or more limbs or is so severely bitten that he or she dies almost immediately, or is carried away and never seen again.

It is very interesting to note that attacks on humans differ in lethality from one geographical area to another. In certain areas the attacks are almost invariably fatal, while in others it is the opposite. The differences can be ascribed to factors like the geography of the area, the depth of the water, the size of the sharks, the types of natural prey in the area, the activity in which the victim is engaged and possibly the water temperature.

We have also found different behaviour patterns in areas that are only 100 kilometres apart, and even in the same area the sharks often behave differently when interacting with one another. The bottom line is that there are no clear-cut rules and parameters regarding shark attacks, or at least none we have discovered so far. So to a large degree we have to assess each attack in its specific context.

We usually assume that a shark attack is a clear-cut, simple event, a surfer or swimmer being attacked by a hungry, vicious shark with nothing left afterwards except bloodstained water and pieces of shredded clothing or wet suit. The truth is not as simple as that. A shark attack is a complex event, consisting of a number of different or interrelated aspects which leave various unanswered questions in their wake.

One of the most perplexing questions is why so many humans survive attacks by great whites. When a white shark launches a full attack on large prey, which might weigh up to 250 kilos, it will feed on the victim once it has been killed. Yet human victims

– who are much more fragile than many sea creatures and weigh far less – usually end up as hospital cases with injuries ranging from very serious to minor cuts and abrasions, and mostly do not die.

So the reasons for, and the dynamics of, shark attacks remain shrouded in mystery, with each painstakingly solved question likely to give birth to a new crop of unanswered ones. The best I can do by way of throwing some light on the subject is to discuss the few existing parameters.

My first example concerns the first 'double' shark attack in South African waters on 14 July 1994 at East London on the east coast – a warm early winter's day with the air temperature at 22 degrees Celsius and the water about 18 degrees Celcius.

Seven surfers were at East London's well-known Nahoon reef breakwater, about 200 metres from the shore, one of them being 31-year-old Andrew Carter. Around half past one that afternoon, Carter was paddling out to the reef after riding a wave to the beach when a great white shark of about 3.5 metres long attacked him from his left.

The shark inflicted serious lacerations to his hip and leg, although no tissue was lost. Carter was lucky enough to be thrown into the sea, leaving the shark swimming in a wide circle while chewing at the board, which was still in its mouth. Then the shark turned and headed back towards Carter, who fended it off after managing to grab the rail of the board on the side opposite to the shark.

The shark then let go of Carter's board and immediately attacked 22-year-old Bruce Corby, who was sitting on his board some 15 metres away. It bit off one of his legs below the knee and disappeared. Other surfers assisted the injured men to shore; Carter survived, but Corby died a few hours later.

A number of actual factors can be identified. The first is that this surfing site can only be described as a high-risk area as far as potential shark attacks are concerned.

The Nahoon reef is situated on a point of headland that extends sharply into the sea and is surrounded by relatively deep water (up to 15 metres), which has a large resident population of fish and rays, and is also frequented by large schools of migrant fish that pass by on a regular basis – on the day in question, in fact, fishermen in the area were catching large numbers of Cape salmon and shad.

Taking all this into account, it is reasonable to assume that the shark was attracted to the abundant food sources in the area, happened to come on the surfers and attacked Carter in the mistaken belief that he was a prey item. That is a reasonable explanation for the shark's first attack, but the reason for the second is less easy to find, since white sharks specifically target their prey and don't blindly strike at whatever happens to be within reach.

So instead of simply assuming that the shark was blood-crazed and willing to attack anything, we need to examine each incident carefully and then apply a little shark psychology to divine why it deviated so significantly from what, as far as we know, is normal behaviour in such circumstances.

As noted elsewhere, white sharks seem to build up immense 'attack energy' before they move in for the kill. In the case of the East London double attack the shark might have been in close proximity to the surfers for some time before picking its target, building up the usual store of attack energy during this period of stalking and selection.

It must be kept in mind that a surfer on a board presents a large prey animal to a 3.5-metre white shark. From Carter's movements while paddling the board the shark obviously knew that its prey was alive. The shark struck, expecting to sink its teeth into living tissue, but instead found itself with a mouthful of foam and glass fibre.

But at the same time there was suddenly a large amount of blood in the water because Carter had been badly hurt during the attack; so, although the shark could not eat what was in its mouth, it would have known that the prey was injured.

Doubtless this left the shark in a state of confusion, which was why it circled Carter with the surfboard still gripped in its mouth. We can also assume that the shark's accumulated attack energy had not been dissipated in 'killing' the surfboard, so it let go of the board and grabbed the next thing that came into its line of vision, namely Bruce Corby's leg.

I have seen this form of blind aggression on many occasions, and the nearest accurate description for it would probably be 'displacement behaviour'. So it seems to me that Bruce Corby was not targeted as a second prey item; like so many other shark victims over the years, he was simply in the wrong place at the wrong time.

What supports this theory is the observed behaviour of great white sharks when they engage in unsuccessful attacks on seals. Once a seal has avoided such an attack the shark almost always turns on anything else that may be in the vicinity, even drifting seaweed or other flotsam, in an apparent effort to displace its pent-up attack energy.

Attacks on divers

In southern African waters, we have recorded several encounters between white sharks and scuba divers, but only one case that resulted in a fatality – Monique Price, who was attacked on the surface at Mossel Bay on 24 June 1990. As I wrote elsewhere in this book, the attack resulted in a strong reaction in the diving community because encounters between white sharks and scuba divers are so rare in South Africa.

White shark attacks on scuba divers are considered very rare elsewhere in the world as well. Great white attacks on scuba, skin and hookah divers are more frequent off north-central California from Point Conception to the Oregon border, though still relatively uncommon. A total of 41 took place between 1952 and 1984, which averages out at 1.3 attacks annually, of which 25 resulted in death or major injury. Of the 41 attacks, 29 (71 per cent of the total) were on divers of one kind or another. Only four attacks involved surface swimmers, and only eight involved surfers or paddle boarders.

The media and certain scientists there claimed that there was an increased incidence of attacks, but although white sharks were often sighted off many of the bathing beaches along this coastline, there was no evidence to suggest any such long-term trend – the number of attacks for this period ranged between zero and seven a year, with most years recording zero, one or occasionally two.

What is a fact, though, is that during the 1960s diving became much more popular and the number of attacks increased slightly in comparison with the 1950s. Every year brought more and more divers into the water, to the point where more than 100 000 scuba divers were registered annually in California, sharing the water with ordinary surface swimmers, free divers, surfers and abalone divers ... and, of course, sharks.

The activities of the divers at the time of the attacks included abalone collecting, spear-fishing and sightseeing. In many cases there was no clarity about the positions of the divers in the water column, but divers were attacked on the bottom, in mid-water and on the surface. In most cases the shark was not seen till the actual attack took place.

To discover the causes of these attacks we have to evaluate each one individually. To make an educated guess, the large number of diver victims was probably due to the fact that white sharks do not venture into the surf-zone, while the divers were in deep water and therefore squarely in the white sharks' domain. The surface attacks we can probably ascribe to the shark in question mistaking the diver for a seal.

California scuba divers sometimes take the precaution of not diving near seal colonies or in places where previous shark attacks have occurred. They also try, where possible, to avoid floating on the surface for unnecessary periods of time. Another evasive tactic among divers is to stay close to cover on the bottom, or to dive in kelp forests.

The risk of shark attacks has apparently had little negative effect on the sport of diving, in California or elsewhere, and each year yet more divers take to the water. So at the risk of repeating myself, the chances of an encounter of the unpleasant kind do not seem at all strong when we consider how many divers make use of the ocean and how few attacks there are.

Attacks on boats

Many attacks on boats have been reported, some provoked and others unprovoked. It is easy to understand provoked attacks, for example a white shark ramming a boat from which it has been harpooned, or when it has a hook and chain embedded in its throat. When you go after a white shark with hook and line or harpoon, you can expect it to retaliate as it fights for its life.

So-called unprovoked attacks are more difficult to analyse, although there is no doubt about the danger involved. White sharks become very large and are capable of inflicting massive damage to very large prey items. That means they are capable of attacking and damaging small boats. That said, the motivation for a white shark to do something as bizarre as attacking a boat for no apparent reason is less clear, since such an act represents an extreme deviation from its natural behaviour.

I have never been involved in any unprovoked attacks, so I am not able to pass qualified judgement, but my empirical knowledge leads me to suggest that 'unprovoked' attacks were, in fact, provoked – it's just that, in most cases at least, the provocation was overlooked or went unnoticed. At the same time I would be the first to admit that that it is possible that some genuinely unprovoked attacks might have occurred, given that white sharks are highly individual and still mysterious creatures.

I can only go by my own experiences and those of my colleagues in the research programme. We have worked with hundreds of white sharks, often from small boats, and have never experienced an unprovoked attack. In addition, we have interviewed hundreds of commercial fishermen who work from small boats in known white shark areas, and they have said that although inquisitive sharks often visited them, none had ever attacked their boats.

Around the Farallon Islands off the northern Californian coast there are enormous white sharks that feed on elephant seals weighing up to a couple thousand kilos, but researchers working off small eight-metre-long Boston whalers often approach to within a few metres of them while they are feeding and have never been attacked. However, there are numerous reports of attacks on boats elsewhere which merit some examination.

In one report from the Azores Islands in the north Atlantic it was recorded that a white shark seven metres in length attacked a six-metre fishing boat, damaging it so severely that it started sinking. The four occupants were rescued and then watched as the shark went to work demolishing their boat altogether.

The details of this reportedly unprovoked attack are sketchy and the attack took place many years ago, so we do not really know what happened. But in spite of the absence of details I am willing to make assumptions that might provide an explanation.

Let us suppose that the four men were catching fish. This would result in signals from the struggling fish and traces of blood in the water from the wounds inflicted by the hooks. Once the fish were hauled onto the boat, they lay there, dripping blood.

If it were a wet deck boat the blood and fluids would slowly have oozed into the water, and the fishermen might have been rinsing the deck and throwing the bloodied water into the ocean. It is also possible that the fishermen were cleaning the fish on the spot and throwing the offal overboard. They might even have been chumming, depending on the type of fish they were after.

Any one of these scenarios might have inadvertently attracted the white shark to their boat through the apparent promise of a free meal, especially if it happened to be hungry. Then, having approached the boat but found little if any actual food, the shark might have become agitated by its frustration, or might even have concluded that the boat was actually the prey because of the food-signals coming from it. The natural consequence to this would have been an attack – mock or serious – on the boat.

One can go further with this hypothesis. Given the era, it would be fair to assume that the boat was made of wood. This raises the possibility that the shark holed the craft, in which case more fish would have been dumped in the water and the shark would have become highly excited, with the panicked movements of the occupants providing even more stimulation.

So if the attack derived from any of the scenarios I have mentioned, it should surely be described as an unintentionally provoked attack, the provocation of which was obscured by panic, excitement, ignorance of great white shark behaviour and, of course, humankind's deeply rooted fear of sharks.

It sounds possible to me. I've said it before and I'll say it again: white sharks are not merely stupid eating machines, and they do not expend energy unnecessarily. That being the case, why would the shark attack an inanimate object for absolutely no reason?

My longtime shark stamping ground, False Bay, can boast more attacks on boats than all the other areas of the world combined. In most cases the attacks were provoked and listed as such, but in some cases they were listed as unprovoked; on investigation into the so-called unprovoked attacks, however, I have come to the conclusion that without exception all the attacks had, in fact, been provoked in one way or another.

The most notorious of these attacks took place in the 1970s, and in this case enough facts are known to eliminate the need for mere assumptions and educated guesses.

Several friends were enjoying a morning's fishing on a six-metre boat in the bay when a large white shark, seemingly for no reason, sprang from the water like a missile and landed in the boat on top of one of the occupants. The unfortunate angler suffered serious injuries and had to be rushed to hospital. *But this was absolutely not an unprovoked attack.*

One of the anglers had hooked a good-sized fish, but when he peered over the side to see what he had caught he spotted a seal pursuing his catch. Not wishing to lose his fish to the seal, he ripped it out of the water. Seals are unbelievably agile swimmers, and when the would-be poacher realised that it had lost its meal it simply did a lightning-like turn on to a new course.

What the angler did not know was that a large, hungry white shark was stalking the seal but couldn't follow it through its sharp turn and so burst out of the water to land squarely in the luckless angler's lap. It is quite evident that the shark had no intention of attacking the boat or the people in it; the entire chain of events was totally accidental.

Needless to say, no such logical explanation appeared in the worldwide flood of scare stories, and great white sharks got another dose of undeserved bad press.

What can I do to stay safe in the water?

As I have said, you are more likely to be killed driving to the beach than being taken out by a shark once you get into the water, but there are certain basic precautions you can take in order to further minimise the chances.

Rescue services in various countries have their own specific protocols, and your best basic rule is to contact the one in the area where you live or are visiting to find out what it would suggest to avoid a shark attack; but local rules apart, here are some precautions you can take:

- Do not swim or surf near seals, or when there is a lot of fish activity. Seals and fish will attract large predators to an area, so if you see lots of activity in the water, rather go to another beach or lie back and catch a tan.

- If you plan to surf it is better to stay away from deep reef or point breaks, which often have a great deal of fish activity, which in turn is likely to attract predators.
- Don't swim or surf in or near rivermouths, which often attract sharks because they know that this is where carrion of various types spills out into the ocean.
- Try to avoid swimming in dirty water. In clear water the shark can easily identify you as something alien and will lose interest, but in dirty water it will use its mouth to investigate possible prey items.
- It is probably a good idea to use brightly coloured equipment like surfboards and wet suits. Sharks often hunt surface-swimming animals like seals or turtles, whose dark colours provide less definition. So by wearing or using equipment in bright colours you will provide more definition for the silhouette the shark sees.
- If you are very concerned about shark attacks, use a larger surfboard. As macro-predators, sharks attack prey smaller than themselves, so the larger the board the greater the likelihood that the shark will go off looking for smaller prey – unless, of course, it is so large itself that even your outsized board looks small by comparison.
- Stay within a group of other water users. The more eyes there are on the surrounding water, the better the chances that someone will spot a shark if it happens to turn up. And, in the worst scenario, there is help at hand if you are unfortunate enough to be attacked.

What should I do in the event of a shark attack?
This is a tough one to answer because there are so many variables, and once again it is always a good idea to contact the relevant rescue services in the area to find out what they would

suggest in the event of a shark attack. But the following are basic steps that apply everywhere:

- Pull the victim away from the shark as soon as possible. This is not as dangerous as it might sound. Experience gained from other attacks shows that the shark is focussed on the victim and does not attack other persons coming to help. There are many cases on record where rescuers have managed to save a victim from under the very nose of the shark and the shark has shown absolutely no interest in them.

- Get the victim out of the water as quickly as possible; once on the beach, place him or her head downwards and wound upwards. Take towels or items of clothing and place them directly onto the wound, then apply very firm pressure on them. If they become saturated with blood, don't remove them – rather place additional items on top of them and keep exerting pressure.

- Make sure that someone has called an ambulance.

- Stop blood-loss as soon as possible and by whatever available means. The leash from a surfboard can be used as a tourniquet, and if something like this is not available, try to place a finger on the severed artery.

- Above all, keep your cool and make sure everyone helping you does likewise; get rid of bystanders. Calm heads save lives, especially if the injuries are serious. A shark attack is a highly charged emotional event for all concerned, with panic, fear and sorrow all rolled instantly into one malign bundle, and in an environment that has suddenly shown itself to be hostile. Whether you are the victim or a Good Samaritan, you must do all you can to remain calm and still, if only because movement can aggravate bleeding or restart it.

TO DIVE OR NOT TO DIVE

For most people the notion of jumping off a perfectly good boat and into a cage bobbing on the waves like a boxer in a ring, surrounded by white sharks weighing in at hundreds and even thousands of kilos, is about as attractive as standing on the wing of a 747 on its final landing approach. Yet more and more people are taking the plunge to come face to face with these powerful and fascinating predators in spite of the tenacious survival of the *Jaws* hysteria.

Right up until the early 1990s the only white shark dive trips available were run out of South Australia; there were plenty of them in southern African waters, but the political isolation of the time ensured that the demand for something similar in South Africa was non-existent.

Things began to change after 1990, and when the campaigning by the South African White Shark Research Institute paid off in April 1991 the white shark received protective legislation in our waters.

For the first time in history the white shark could roam a piece of the ocean without the threat of being hunted, and this news immediately attracted huge international interest from documentary companies.

For the next three years the institute hosted no less than a dozen international documentary film crews, so that when the remnants of apartheid collapsed after the 1994 general election the world knew that we had lots of white sharks – and the world wanted to see them. Our sharks were easily accessible, and we could take divers to see these animals at a fraction of the price of the Australian operators, who were asking up to US$800 per day per person.

The tourist demand for white shark experiences and the local demand for foreign currency caused the diving industry to mushroom virtually overnight, with every Tom, Dick and Harry who owned a boat and a welding machine turning himself into a dive operator. Inevitably the results were disastrous, with poor service, dangerous operational practices and a great deal of infighting the order of the day.

The situation eventually became so serious that the Department of Fisheries stepped in and threatened to close the new industry down if it did not pull itself out of its self-created mess. It helped that the world had become a great deal smaller than it was. News of bad operators spread like wildfire, forcing them either to close shop or improve their services, and, over time, the industry achieved levels of international service.

Nowadays over 30 000 tourists pay to go out and see the great white sharks of South Africa each year; and parallel industries have developed in the United States, New Zealand and Mexico to service a demand which just keeps growing.

Shark-diving is not universally accepted, however. Certain surfers, conservationists and general water users are staunchly opposed to it, their main objection being the belief that the chumming that lays out an odour corridor to attract the sharks is conditioning them to associate human divers in cages with food. I believe that this is wrong, as wrong as the assumption that chumming conditions sharks to attack bathers and surfers, and I offer two reasons.

Firstly, white sharks, unlike many other shark species, are highly nomadic and usually do not spend more than days or weeks in one area, which would surely not give them enough time to become conditioned.

Secondly, and this is a more substantial argument, white sharks probably cannot distinguish between the cage and the diver inside, or mentally separate the one from the other. The shark simply sees the boat, the cage attached to it and the diver as one large, very strange object.

Even if the shark was able to distinguish between diver and cage, the fact that it ends up with a mouthful of unappetising steel when it bites would, if anything, teach it that divers are not edible. The situation is very much like the reaction of a lion to an open game-viewing vehicle. The lion does not mentally separate the occupants from the vehicle; it simply perceives one large strange object which is not an obvious prey item, and so it has little interest in either the vehicle or its occupants.

Some people have also speculated that dive tours increase the chances of shark attacks at nearby beaches, and that there is some kind of connection between sharks feeding out at sea and shark attacks. But there is absolutely no basis for this speculation at all. Sharks have been attracted to fishing boats for as long as men have been fishing, taking fish off the lines or nosing around in the chum slick. There is no evidence that these fishing boats have ever been responsible for a shark attacking a bather at a beach, and obviously the same would apply to a dive boat.

It has also been argued that shark-diving changes the shark's natural behaviour. This may be true with certain resident shark species, but there is no evidence to support this claim when it comes to great white sharks. The South African Department of Sea Fisheries and Marine and Coastal Management have been conducting extensive research projects into the question of sharks' behaviour changes, and at the time of writing they have found absolutely no evidence of such changes in the great white shark population.

In a nutshell, white sharks are still doing exactly the same things as they were doing a decade ago.

So the question is whether shark-diving is good or bad. We feel that shark-diving is good for several reasons if it is conducted under the correct conditions and by professionals who have a sincere interest in the animals.

Firstly, professionally conducted shark-viewing – whether underwater or on the surface – is very educational, possibly one of the most awe-inspiring experiences on the planet today. You can't help being seduced by great whites, and in our experience even the strongest anti-shark attitudes tend to change remarkably after a day or two in the company of these magnificent animals. On top of that, well-managed dive tours are very safe and one almost never hears of accidents.

Secondly, sharks have become the number one diving attraction around the world, and because diving is one of the fastest growing sports in the world, sharks are now far more valuable alive than dead. A great white shark which would have fetched several hundred dollars as a dead carcass less than a decade ago is now a valuable non-consumable resource capable of generating tens of thousands of dollars per year for as long as it is alive and well.

Thirdly, dedicated divers, tourists, environmentalists or conservationists who go out on a shark trip enjoy themselves in the knowledge that they are not only not harming the environment but are supporting an industry that has a vested interest in protecting the species.

Sharks of every species need all the support they can get. Totally uncontrolled shark hunting takes place on an unprecedented scale almost everywhere in the world, so that an estimated 100 million sharks disappear from the world's oceans each year. Many shark species are literally at the point of no recovery; the numbers of mako, blue, white and porbeagle sharks, to name just a few, for example, are down by 90 per cent in the North Atlantic Ocean alone, and this seems to be par for the course in most other ocean areas.

The only lasting solution is a situation in which sharks are more valuable alive than dead, and we should all seize every opportunity to make it happen. One small but telling blow you can strike is to heed your moral obligation to make sure that you are taken out by an ethical, honest operator ... *and think twice about ever buying any shark products.*

And shark-diving does not end with white sharks. Depending on where you go in the world, you can dive with hammerhead, reef, bull, tiger, mako, blue and whale sharks, to name only some. The operators on most of these dives do not use chumming and baiting, making their activities about as near to pure ecotourism as it is possible to get, and the more people support them, the

Last word: Sharks, the real victims

The world's sharks are disappearing so quickly that I actually feel panic at the thought of what is going to happen if they are not afforded worldwide protection. In this spirit, I end my book with a gut-wrenching story. If you are squeamish, don't read it. But try to make the effort. It is an accurate description of a tragedy that happens many times every day in one or other place in the world, and which will soon reduce our 500-odd shark species by half if something is not done.

She was breathtakingly beautiful as her four-metre-long body rose towards the surface of the Indian Ocean, each of her intricate markings clearly visible in the crystal-pure water.

She was an Alopias vulpinus, *the largest of the thresher shark family, with a tail that was just as long as her muscular body and far more lethal than her small, harmless jaws. Although she looked very big, her body was only two metres wide because she was still young; it would be several more years before she was sexually mature, able to mate and give birth to three infants.*

Her bluish-green back broke the surface of the calm ocean under the uninterested gaze of an albatross gliding overhead. She could not understand why she was unable to return to the depths, or why the small inconspicuous piece of sardine she had swallowed was causing her such pain. For several hours she had been fighting against something impaled deep in her throat, but now she was too exhausted even to panic and too weak to fight any longer against whatever it was that had attacked her.

Two metres above her, the most efficient and deadly predator on earth took careful aim and then struck with perfect precision. The steel talons pierced her soft skin and sank deep into the back of her neck, sending a jolt of pain through her limp body as she was hauled roughly out of the water for the final indignity.

The predator had no time to waste on her because the hunt was still on, so the steely grip relaxed and let her tumble to the cold, blood-soaked deck of the 3 000-ton factory ship. The impact of the fall extinguished what little strength remained in her, and she lay motionless on her side with one eye submerged in the blood of her fellow victims.

Strange noises could be heard around her, the voices of men laughing and joking as they walked around in her blood. Then one of the men grabbed her beautiful long tail that had propelled her through the oceans for nine years and slashed it off with a quick flash of steel. Her high dorsal fin and two big pectoral fins followed. In only a few moments she had been reduced from a magnificent oceanic predator to a mutilated, useless, barely living carcass.

There was no more pain now as the life ebbed from her, and she barely felt the two steel hooks that came down to pierce her body, or the rough deck over which she was dragged towards the side of the ship, where two men started pushing and kicking her overboard like the piece of debris she had become.

A moment later she fell back into the familiar blue world in which she spent her life, and which now became her grave as she slowly floated down to the depths and died ...

There would be a worldwide outcry if rabbits or dogs, cats or lions were to be caught, mutilated and then discarded to die slowly and painfully, merely so that their paws could be used to make soup served as a delicacy for the wealthy. But every year there is a massive slaughter of sharks – living creatures just like them – and there is hardly a protesting voice.

The true horror of this story is that a shark is innocent of all wrongdoing or evil intentions. When it is hungry its instincts tell it to eat and satisfy that hunger. There is no cognitive process involved, no ethical debate and no waste unless the prey is too large for the shark to consume entirely, or it is scared off for some reason or other.

But humankind, with our large brains and finely honed thinking processes, will kill a shark for its fins alone and let the rest rot away, to the detriment of the species and ultimately the entire ocean – not to survive, but to make money by selling the gruesome relics for rich connoisseurs' dining tables.

One of the cornerstones of jurisprudence is the principle that a person is fit for trial if, at the time of committing a crime, he or she was capable of understanding that it was a criminal act.

It is a question that we should, perhaps, be asking ourselves.